SURVIVAL FITNESS

THE ULTIMATE FITNESS PLAN FOR ESCAPE, EVASION, AND SURVIVAL

SAM FURY

Illustrated by
SHUMONA MALLICK, OKIANG LUHUNG,
RAUL GUAJARDO, AND YOPI MUHAMAD

CONTENTS

ESSENTIAL PARKOUR TRAINING

BASIC ROCK CLIMBING

SURVIVAL SWIMMING

EFFICIENT SWIMMING

MOUNTAIN BIKE RIDING

HIKING

WARNINGS AND DISCLAIMERS

The information in this publication is made public for reference only.

Neither the author, publisher, nor anyone else involved in the production of this publication is responsible for how the reader uses the information or the result of his/her actions.

Consult a physician before undertaking any new form of physical activity.

INTRODUCTION

This book (Survival Fitness) is self-training in the 5 most useful activities for escaping danger.

The idea is that if you are going to exercise, you may as well learn life-saving skills at the same time.

It is the ultimate in functional fitness training.

Survival Fitness includes full versions of Sam Fury's:

- Daily Health and Fitness
- Essential Parkour
- Basic Rock-climbing
- Survival Swimming

It also ads hiking and mountain bike riding.

The point of Survival Fitness is not to be a master in all the activities. Although this is possible, it takes a lot of training and most people will not have the time or motivation.

Instead, the aim is to increase fitness and skill to an above average level (in comparison to the general population) in all of the activities. This will give you best overall chance of survival when in danger.

DAILY HEALTH AND FITNESS

INTRODUCTION

Daily Health and Fitness is a complete body and mind health routine consisting of 4 parts.

Do all 4 parts every day for optimal health.

1. **Nutrition.** What you put into your body matters, a lot.
2. **Body Conditioning.** Two extremely efficient exercises to keep your whole body strong, including the awesome SFP Super-burpee.
3. **Yoga Stretch Routine.** Stretch your whole body using this specially designed 15-minute yoga routine.
4. **Yoga Nidra.** A quick Yoga Nidra session as a form of daily meditation.

Nutrition is observed at all times.

If you do the other 3 things "back to back" it takes less than 45 minutes. They can also be easily split up throughout the day to suit your schedule.

Be diligent in the above and in under 45 minutes a day you will be healthier in body and mind **than the majority of people on the planet!**

NUTRITION

These Survival Fitness Plan nutrition guidelines are easy to remember to stick with.

There are 5 major guidelines:

1. Fast for 16 hours a day
2. Eat gut healthy food
3. Eat a plant-based whole-foods diet
4. Minimize refined sugar
5. Minimize drug use

16 Hour Fasting

This is intermittent fasting. There are several ways to do it but I find this one way the best because it becomes part of your daily routine. It keeps things simple.

The times you choose depends on your lifestyle, as long as it is 16 hours. I like to fast between 8 pm and 12 noon the following day. All I am doing is skipping breakfast.

During the fasting period you can drink water, herbal tea, or black coffee. If you get hungry try having a tablespoon of apple cider vinegar in a glass of water. A tablespoon of coconut oil is also good. You should consume these two things every day anyway. Both are good for your health.

Intermittent fasting has some great benefits such as:

- Boosts immune system.
- Fat loss.
- Improves longevity.
- Lowers risk if diabetes.
- Reduces risk of cancer (non yet proven).

- Sleep better.
- Slows aging.
- Think clearer.

Eat Gut Healthy Food

A healthy gut is a healthy mind and body.

This is a scientific fact!

There are many food that are good for your guts. Kefir is one of the best, but if that's not your thing then any fermented foods are good too.

Apple cider vinegar, sauerkraut, kimchi, tempeh, miso, and pickles are all good examples.

Also eat foods that are high in fiber such as whole grains, beans, legumes, and whole fruits and veggies.

Aim to get a good dose of high fiber and fermented foods every day.

Plant Based Whole Foods

What are whole foods? Here is a definition straight from Wikipedia:

"Whole foods are plant foods that are unprocessed and unrefined, or processed and refined as little as possible, before being consumed. Examples of whole foods include whole grains, tubers, legumes, fruits, vegetables."

https://en.wikipedia.org/wiki/Whole_food

As a bonus, eating a whole foods diet will cut your food bill. Quite a lot in some cases.

Anything made with white flour is not a whole food. Includes bread, cereals, crackers, granola bars, pasta, etc. You can still eat these things but choose the non-white whole grain version instead.

Same goes for white rice. Eat wild or brown rice instead.

"Normal" potatoes are okay but sweet potatoes are way better.

Here's a list of no white-flour foods.

www.LiveStrong.com/article/336585-list-of-no-white-flour-foods

Eat Less Refined Sugar

Refined sugar is poison and is in many things. Here are some examples. The less of these things you eat, the healthier you will be.

Processed Food. Almost everything processed will have refined sugar in it. This covers most things that are not in the "fresh-food" section of the supermarket. The easiest way to know is by looking at the ingredients label.

Deep Fried Foods. Most things that are deep-fried will also have refined sugar. Even if they don't, nothing deep fried is good for you anyway.

Drinks. Drinks other than water and fresh herbal tea usually have quite a bit of sugar in them. Soft drinks are the worst.

Clean water is the best drink you can have. Making it your main drink will flush your body of toxins. Aim to drink AT LEAST one liter every day.

Herbal teas, either cold or hot brewed, are a good way to add a bit of flavor as well as get some extra benefits.

Every morning when you wake, rinse your mouth out and then drink a couple of cups of water. It will assist rehydration from the night and stimulate your digestive system.

Minimize Drug Use

This includes alcohol, cigarettes, pharmaceuticals you don't need, and illicit drugs.

Of course, some drugs are worse than others. Smoking cigarettes, for example, is crazy. Drinking a little alcohol once in a while, not so bad.

The antibiotics prescribed to clear an infection you should probably continue to take. The anti-depressants your psychiatrist gave you I would consider flushing down the toilet.

Additional Healthy Eating Tips

Fruits. Fruits are great but due to a large amount of fructose consuming too much is bad for your teeth. Limit yourself to three serves a day. High fructose corn syrup is much more harmful to your health than regular fruit fructose.

Vegetables. You cannot eat too many vegetables. They should make up a big part of your diet. Local fruits and vegetables that are in season for your location are best.

Herbs. Not only do they make your food taste nicer, they are super healthy. Garlic, ginger, and chili are my favorites, and they are very cheap to buy and easy to grow. Garlic is crazy healthy.

Fresh salads, soups, or steamed are the best way to prepare your vegetables. The next best is stir-fried, roasted, etc. Stay away from anything shallow or deep fried.

Bright or deep colors are best. Go for leafy greens, berries, red bell peppers, papaya, moringa, etc.

Wash all fruits and vegetables. Even organic fruits and vegetables can have poison sprayed on them. Also, ensure you use water you would consider safe to drink.

Get a good variety. Different foods have different nutritional value. When it comes to fruit and vegetables, choose a variety of colors and types. This actually applies to all food. Ensure you are consuming proteins, dairy, fruit, vegetables, complex carbohydrates, good fats, etc.

Proteins. Vegetarian proteins (tofu, eggs, beans, etc.) are best for health and other reasons. Failing that, go for fish (salmon is great) and lean meats (skinless chicken and lean beef are my favorites).

When you crave something sweet go for dark chocolate. The higher percentage of cocoa the better. Raw Honey is also great.

Benefits of Being Vegetarian

For those that think you need meat for a balanced diet, you are incorrect. There are lots of replacement options such as tofu, legumes, nuts, eggs, etc.

There's a few of reasons I advocate vegetarianism.

- It's healthier. Much healthier than most people realize.
- The animal cruelty factor, especially with factory farming. Even better on this front would be to go vegan.
- It saves money. In most cases, being vegetarian is cheaper than eating meat.

Here's a link to a documentary called "Mad Cowboy". It is worth the watch:

www.youtube.com/watch?v=piZmH4gzyqs

LIFE FORCE

Life force is a non-physical essential energy which is present throughout all things in the universe, and the universe provides it in abundance for all.

Although the concept of life force is rejected by modern science, the notion of it is present in most cultures, both east and west.

Depending on where you are from, you may know it as Chi, Élan vital, Gi, Khi, Ki, Manitou, Prana, Ruah, Qi, Vitalism, etc.

In relation to living creatures, this essential energy flows through the body. If it gets blocked, the symptoms of the blockage are manifested as illness and/or pain.

This means that any "sickness" you have, whether it be physical, mental, emotional, etc. is caused by blocked energy, and can therefore be alleviated by releasing the blockage.

It also means that sickness can be prevented by maintaining clear passages of this energy through the body.

The simplest way to encourage and maintain the flow of this energy through the body is the breath.

Life Force and the Breath

Although every breath you take helps to circulate the life force throughout your body, taking "full" breaths is much more effective.

Unfortunately, most people do not take full breaths.

When you take the time to concentrate on proper breathing it will promote better breathing overall, i.e., even when you are not concentrating on it.

It takes a cycle of 9 breathes for the first breath to be exhaled from the body. It is recommended to do 4 cycles of conscious breathing a day. This can be done all at once (36 breathes) or 9 at a time at various times during the day.

Doing the Yoga Stretch Routine will cover 36 conscious breaths and then some. But you can do them whenever you want. The more the better.

If you only want to do one thing a day to maintain your health, do conscious breathing.

Receiving the Breath

Get in a comfortable position, e.g., lying, sitting, standing. Completely exhale your whole breath. This is the "effort" part.

Now just allow the inhale to come in naturally through your nose. There is no need to actively breathe in deeply. Just receive it. Over time you will notice that your breaths naturally get deeper.

As you breathe in and out it may help to imagine the flow of energy carried by your breath. It comes up your back as you inhale, and down your front as you exhale.

Inhale in all the goodness of new a positive energy, exhale all the stale and negative.

Three Part Breath

This is the breath you should do when actively practicing yoga, but when first learning it you will probably just want to do it from a sitting or lying position.

Breathe in long and deep through your nose. First feel it enter your lower belly, then your lower chest/rib cage, and finally into your lower throat/top of sternum. Feel the clear, positive energies of happiness and love come up from your toes to you head.

When you are ready, exhale fully through your nose, feeling it leave in the opposite order it came in, i.e., first from your sternum, then your chest, and finally your belly. Release all negative energy and tension out of your body from your head to your toes.

Continue to breathe in and out like this, smooth and continuous.

When you first start to practice this type of breathing it may help to put your hands on each of the three areas as you do it, i.e. belly, chest, and sternum. You can also try just breathing into each area on its own.

BODY CONDITIONING

Described in this section are two exercises designed to keep your physical body strong in the most efficient way.

5 SFP super-burpees is the bare minimum of daily exercise.

The ideal daily conditioning routine is:

- 10 SFP super-burpees.
- 10 pull-ups.

Super-Burpees

The Survival Fitness Plan (SFP) super-burpee is an extremely efficient exercise which acts as a warm-up, light stretch, and full body muscle conditioning workout all in one.

When done properly and in succession they also serve to fill the body with life force as well as give a cardio-vascular work out.

Furthermore, it has been tweaked over time to give additional benefits in relation to SFP Fight and Flight activities such as parkour and self-defense.

Here is a list of the main benefits gained from the SFP super-burpee:

- Balance.
- Cardiovascular workout.
- Circulation of life force.
- Coordination.
- Explosiveness.
- Improve bodily functions (digestion, respiratory, etc.)
- Flexibility.
- Muscle conditioning.

- Hang time (the ability to stay airborne).
- Striking strength and speed.
- Warm-up.

It is highly recommended to do **AT LEAST** 5 SFP super-burpees every morning to ready your body for the day.

One SFP super-burpee takes less than 10 seconds.

Even if you only have one minute to spare for exercise, you have time to do SFP super-burpees!

It is also recommended to do SFP super-burpees as a general warm-up before any vigorous exercise, such as SFP Fight and Flight training.

The SFP super-burpee is made up of five separate exercises, and each of these exercises have been specifically chosen and tweaked to get the most out of them in relation to the Survival Fitness Plan.

Jumping Squats: Jumping squats develop leg strength, core strength, explosiveness, soft landing skills, jumping ability, and hang-time.

Finger-tip Push-ups: Finger-tip push-ups increase finger strength and grip, increases striking power, and improve all over body conditioning.

Clapping Push-ups: Being a push-up these are great for increasing striking power and all over body conditioning. The clapping part really improves explosiveness which is awesome for speed and power. They also condition your hands for the palm heel strike which is preferred over a fist in SFP Self-Defense Training.

Hindu Push-ups: Hindu push-ups uses the downward dog and the upward dog (yoga poses) which are beneficial for:

- Brain (stimulates).

- Breathing (chest).
- Concentration.
- Eyesight.
- Hearing.
- Kidneys.
- Memory.
- Nervous system.
- Spine.
- Whole body strengthening.

Brazilians: Brazilians mainly contribute to cardiovascular workout and hip flexibility, but they also increase core strength and work the lower abdominals.

If you are unable to do a full SFP super-burpee you can build yourself up to them by doing each individual exercise separately.

Once you can do each 10 repetitions of each individual exercise you should be strong enough to put them together into a SFP super-burpee.

The first SFP super-burpee you do for the day (or when warming up for exercise) must be done slowly and with much purpose.

If you try to do fast super-burpees straight away chances of injury greatly increase. By doing the first one very well it will warm-up and stretch your body. After that you can gradually increase speed with the second and third repetitions until you are going full-speed for as many reps as you can handle.

Note: If you have any injuries please leave out any part of the SFP super-burpee that may aggravate it.

The following is a detailed explanation of how to do a full SFP super-burpee as if it is the first one.

Jumping Squat

Stand straight with your feet shoulder width apart.

As you breathe in, squat down as low as you can. Keep your back straight and come up on your toes as you squat down. Put your arms out to your front. This will help you keep your back straight.

Spring up as you exhale and jump as high as you can. Tuck your legs up as high as possible on the outside of your elbows. Try to keep your back straight. This is actually a box jump.

Land as softly as you can and adopt a crouching squat position.

Note: If you cannot do a jumping squat you can build up to them by doing regular squats first. Just do as explained above but without the jump.

Finger-tip Push-up

From the squat position, as you inhale, place your finger-tips firmly on the ground next to your feet and shoot both your legs behind you so you are in the standard up position of a push-up, with the exception of being on your finger-tips.

Ensure that your elbows are as close to your torso as possible and that they are facing back towards your feet. This is so you target the muscles used for striking.

Grip the floor with your fingers, as if you are trying to rip a chunk out of the ground. Keep this grip throughout the push-up.

As you inhale, lower your chest until your arms are at a 90° angle at the elbow.

Push back up as fast as possible to the up position.

Clapping Push-up

Lower your chest again as you inhale.

This time, as you exhale, push-up hard enough for you to be able to get your hands off the ground and clap.

Aim to land on the palms of your hands as softly as possible and then return to the up position of the push-up.

Note: If you cannot do either of these push-ups, work your way up to them with normal push-ups i.e. on your hands. Next do finger-tip pushups, and then clapping pushups.

If you cannot yet do a normal push-up, work your way up to it first by lying on your stomach and pushing up.

Push on the ground for 10 seconds and then rest. This is one rep. Do three sets of three reps every day. Eventually you will be able to do a push-up. Once you can do 10 normal push-ups, try for finger-tip pushups.

It will help to do finger strengthening exercises also. A simple and very effective one is to place your fingers tips together and push them against each-other for as long as you can. Do it every day until you are able to do finger-tip push-ups.

Hindu Push-up

From the up position of the push-up breathe in and go into downward dog. See the yoga section for a detailed description of the downward dog.

If this is your first SFP super-burpee, spend a couple of breaths here to stretch your body. Go up on each foot to stretch your legs and really extend your upper body.

When ready, as you breathe out, sweep down in a circular arc motion into upward dog. See the yoga section for a detailed description of the upward dog.

Again, if this is your first SFP super-burpee, spend a couple of breaths here to stretch your body.

Really arch your back and look high above. Move your neck from side to side and stretch out your arms, back, and upper thighs.

When you are ready, inhale and return to the up position of the push-up.

Brazilians

As you exhale bring your right knee to your left elbow and then back. Then bring your left knee to your right elbow. This is one rep of a Brazilian.

Jump your feet back into a squat and then stand up straight.

This completes one repetition of a SFP super-burpee.

A complete SFP super-burpee

Pull-ups

Being able to pull yourself up is an extremely useful skill and the best way to condition your self is with the the classic pull-up.

The pull-up is an especially useful exercise for parkour so you can build strength for wall-climbs and eventually muscle-ups.

Grab the bar with a grip slightly wider than shoulder width apart and with your palms facing away from you.

Let yourself hang all the way down.

Pull yourself up by pulling your shoulder-blades down and together. Keep your chest up and pull up until your chin is above the bar. Touch your chest on it.

As you are pulling up keep your body in a vertical line. Do not swing. Concentrate on isolating your back and biceps.

Pause at the top and then lower yourself back down to the hanging position.

YOGA STRETCH ROUTINE

Note: If you are planning to do more physical exercise as part of this routine, do it after conditioning and before this yoga stretch routine.

The information in this section is from the book Curing Yoga by Aventuras De Viaje.

www.SurvivalFitnessPlan.com/Curing-Yoga

The SFP Yoga Cool-Down is a whole body stretch which also gives the many other benefits of yoga. Balance, a calm mind, coordination, core strength, development of chi, flexibility, etc.

This yoga cool-down is approximately 15 minutes long if you stay in each pose for 2 to 3 breaths.

The longer you stay in each pose for, the more beneficial it is, so go longer than 15 minutes if you want.

Note: Other than the first time they appear, table and staff poses are transitional. When doing a 15-minute routine only stay in them for a few seconds.

Whilst doing this routine it is important to move slowly and use conscious breathing.

The poses used in this yoga cool-down are of a basic level, but some of them can still be challenging at the start. Adjust them to your comfort level and build your way up. Hold each pose where you can feel a good stretch but not pain.

You will notice your breath shorten if you try to force your body too much. When this happens, back of a little and re-focus on your breathing.

If you do find yourself in a painful position, ease out of it to avoid injury.

At the end of this chapter is a "quick list" of the poses which you can print out/photocopy for easy reference.

MOUNTAIN POSE
Avoid if you have a shoulder injury.

Stand with your feet parallel and either together or hip-width apart.

Spread your toes wide and balance your weight and central over each foot.

Pull up your kneecaps and tense your thighs. Keep your legs straight but do not lock your knees.

Ensure your hips are over your ankles.

As you inhale, lengthen your spine so that the crown of your head goes straight up towards the sky.

When you exhale drop your shoulders and lengthen your finger-tips towards the ground. Keep extending your head upwards.

At the same time direct your chest straight ahead.

Continue to lengthen through your finger-tips. Inhale and bring your arms up above your head. Reach for the sky with your palms facing each other.

As you exhale, relax your shoulders but continue to lengthen your crown and fingers to the sky.

An alternative is to interlace your fingers with your index fingers pointing up.

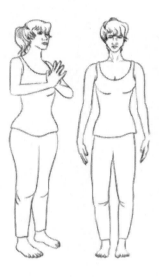

When you are ready, exhale as you bring your palms together in front of your chest in a prayer position. Take a breath and on the exhale allow your hands to drop to your sides.

STANDING BACK BEND
Avoid if you have a back, hip, and/or neck injury.

As you breathe in, place the palms of your hands on your lower back (sacrum) with your fingers pointing to the ground.

Squeeze your buttocks and thighs tight, pull up your kneecaps, and press into your feet.

Exhale as you press your hips forward to arch your back.

You can either look straight ahead or allow your head to drop all the way back.

Increase the stretch by walking your hands down the back of your legs.

Ease back into a standing position with your hands by your sides.

CRESCENT MOON

Avoid if you have a back, hip, and/or shoulder injury.

While inhaling, adopt mountain pose. Interlace your fingers and point your index fingers to the sky.

As you exhale, press your left hip out to the side and arch to your right. Keep your body strong and lengthened.

Inhale as you return to center. Repeat it on your other side.

STANDING FORWARD FOLD

Avoid if you have a back, hip, leg, and/or shoulder injury.

Exhale and bring your head to your knees with your palms flat on the floor.

Stretch your spine by pulling your head down while pushing your hips up. Bend your knees if you need to but aim to be able to do it with straight legs.

Press your belly into your thighs when inhaling.

For a deeper stretch hold the back of your calves and pull your head closer to your legs.

TABLE POSE

Avoid if you have a knee and/or wrist injury.

As you inhale, place your hands and knees on the floor.

Your palms underneath your shoulders and fingers facing forwards.

Ensure your knees are shoulder width apart and your feet are behind them. The tops of your feet and toes are on the floor.

Look at the ground between your hands and press down into your palms.

Have your back flat and exhale.

Lengthen your spine by pressing the crown of your head forward and your tailbone back.

THREADING THE NEEDLE

Avoid if you have a knee, neck, and/or shoulder injury.

As you exhale, slide your right hand between your left knee and left hand. Aim for your right shoulder and the side of your head to rest on the floor.

Inhale and reach towards the sky with your left hand.

Find where you get the deepest stretch and stay there. Reach out through your fingers.

When ready, exhale as you bring your hand back to the floor and then inhale to readopt table pose.

Repeat on your left side.

UPWARD DOG

Avoid if you have an arm, back, hip, and/or shoulder injury, and/or have had recent abdominal surgery, and/or are pregnant.

Drop your hips forward towards the ground as you press your palms down into the floor.

Press your chest forward and drop your shoulders down and back. Push the crown of your head towards the ceiling.

As you inhale press the tops of your feet into the ground to lift your legs off the floor.

Only the tops of your feet and your hands touch the ground. Press your toenails into the floor.

Note: If you did SFP Super-Burpees before this yoga routine you can skip upward dog and downward dog.

DOWNWARD DOG

Avoid if you have an arm, back, hip, and/or shoulder injury, and/or unmediated high blood pressure.

Inhale as you tuck your toes so you are on the balls of your feet. Keep your palms shoulder-width apart. Spread your fingers apart with your middle fingers facing forward.

Press into your hands and lift your hips towards the sky.

Push your hips up and back. Your chest goes towards your thighs. Have straight arms but do not lock your elbows.

Keep your spine straight as you lift up through your tailbone.

Stretch the back of your legs by pressing your heels to the floor. Keep your back flat. Your legs are straight (knees not locked) or with a small bend at the knees.

Let your head dangle free.

Move back into table pose.

LOW WARRIOR

Avoid if you have an ankle, arm, hip, and/or shoulder injury.

Step your right foot forward, placing it in-between your hands. Your knee is over your ankle.

Ensure your left knee and left and right feet are firm on the ground and then place your hands on your right knee.

Straighten your arms and bring your torso back. Do not lock your elbows.

Relax your shoulders and bring your shoulder blades towards each other. This is to stick out your chest.

As you inhale, raise your arms over your head with your palms facing each other and arch your back as you look up to the sky.

If this is difficult then you can keep your hands on your bent knee.

Exhale as you bring your palms back to the floor on either side of your right foot.

HALF PRAYER TWIST

Avoid if you have a back, hip, knee, and/or shoulder injury.

As you inhale bring your torso up and place your hands together in a prayer position.

Put your right elbow on the outside of your left knee and use your arms to press your right shoulder up and back. Feel it twist your upper back.

Ensure your palms remain in the center of your chest. Your fingers point towards your throat.

You can either look straight ahead or up towards the sky.

Exhale as you bring your palms back to the floor on either side of your right foot.

HALF PYRAMID
Avoid if you have a knee and/or leg injury.

While still exhaling straighten your right leg and press your hips toward your left heel.

Round your spine and lift your toes to the sky as you push your forehead to your right knee.

Walk your hands back towards you to support your torso.

Relax your elbows, face, neck, and shoulders.

Inhale and bend your right knee back over your ankle. Then exhale and bring your right knee back into table position.

Do low warrior, half prayer twist, and half pyramid on your left side.

EXTENDED DOG POSE

Avoid if you have an arm, back, knee, and/or shoulder injury.

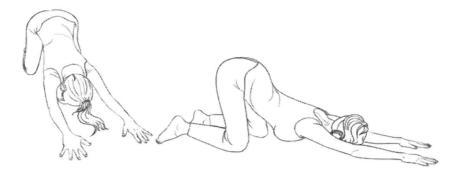

As you inhale push your tailbone towards the sky. Exhale and lower your forehead to the floor by sliding your hands forward. Keep your hips lifted over your knees.

Arch the middle of your back by allowing your chest to sink towards the floor.

You can deepen the stretch also. Straighten your arms, lift your elbows off the floor, and bring your hips back. Try not to let your hands slide while you do this.

Place your chin on the ground to stretch your neck.

Inhale and return to the table position.

HERO POSE

Bring your knees together with your feet hip-width apart. Sit with your bum on the ground and your heels on the outside of your hips.

If this is too difficult you can sit on your heels.

Place your hands on your knees. Your palms can face up or down.

Lengthen your torso by reaching the crown of your head to the sky.

Push your lower legs into the ground, drop your shoulders, and press your chest forward.

Relax your belly, face, jaw, and tongue.

Hero pose is an excellent pose to rest and/or for meditation.

LION POSE

Avoid if you have a face, knee, neck, and/or tongue injury.

Bring your feet together and spread your knees as wide as you comfortably can. Sit on your heels.

Inhale and lengthen your spine by reaching the crown of your head to the sky.

Bring your palms to the floor in-between your knees with your fingers facing your body.

Arch your spine, stick your tongue out and exhale via your mouth ferociously.

Repeat this a few times.

DOWNWARD FACING FROG

Avoid if you have a knee, hip, and/or leg injury.

Keep your knees where they are and align your feet so that they are behind them. Right foot behind right knee and left foot behind left knee.

Turn your feet outwards so your toes are facing away from your body.

Place your elbows, forearms, and palms flat on the floor.

Exhale as you push your hips back.

When ready bring your hips forward and place your palms under your shoulders to adopt table pose.

STAFF POSE

Move into a seated position with your legs extended straight out in front of you.

Place your hands beside your hips with your fingers pointed forward.

Lengthen your spine by pressing your hip bones down. Push the crown of your head towards the sky.

Use your arms for support as you push your chest forward and lower your shoulders.

Pull your toes towards your head as you push your heels away from you.

SEATED FORWARD BEND

Avoid if you have an ankle, arm, hip, and/or shoulder injury.

Inhale and raise your arms up to the sky with your palms facing each other. Lengthen your torso through your fingers and the crown of your head.

As you exhale bend at the hips, lowering your upper body to your legs. Grab your ankles, feet, or toes.

Push out through your heels as you pull your toes back towards you.

You can also use your arms to pull yourself closer to your legs. For those with more flexibility reach your hands in front of your feet.

If you are having difficulties bend your knees enough so you can reach your feet and place your head on your knees.

Roll up your spine back into staff pose.

BOUND ANGLE

Avoid if you have a hip and/or knee injury.

Bend your legs to bring the bottoms of your feet together. Your knees bend facing out.

Hold onto your toes by interlacing your fingers around them.

As you inhale stretch the crown of your head up towards the sky while pushing your hips down.

Push your chest forward and relax your shoulders down.

Close your eyes and look to your third eye (behind the middle of your forehead).

As you exhale push your knees to the ground and pull your torso forward. Ensure to keep your chest open and back flat.

For a deeper stretch pull your forehead or chest towards your feet.

Return to staff pose.

SEATED ANGLE

Avoid if you have an arm, hip, knee, and/or shoulder injury.

As you inhale spread your legs out as wide as comfortable. Ensure your knees and toes are pointing up and reach through your fingers up to the sky.

Exhale as you lower your palms to the floor. Deepen the stretch by walking your hands forward. Stay focused on keeping your spine long.

You could also hold your big toes and use them to help pull your torso down.

When ready inhale and walk your hands in as your roll back your spine until finishing with a straight back.

SIDE SEATED ANGEL

Avoid if you have a hip, leg, and/or lower back injury.

Turn to face your right foot by twisting at your waist.

Walk your hands towards your right foot as you exhale. Try to reach your forehead to your knee and hold your right ankle or foot if you are able.

Relax your shoulders and neck, then increase the stretch. Press your heel out while pulling your toes back towards yourself.

Return to the center with your back straight and then do the same thing on your left side.

Return to the staff position.

JOYFUL BABY

Avoid if you have a leg, neck, and/or shoulder injury.

As you inhale bring your knees to your chest.

Weave your arms through the inside of your knees and hold onto the pinkie toe side edges of your feet.

Keep your head on the ground and tuck your chin to your chest.

Push your heels up to the sky as you pull back with your arms. At the same time press the back of your neck, shoulders, sacrum, and tailbone to the floor.

Open your legs wider for a deeper hip stretch.

Exhale and roll your spine back to the ground until you are lying flat again.

WIND RELIEVING POSE

Avoid if you have a hernia and/or have had recent abdominal surgery.

As you inhale bring both knees up to your chest. Hug your knees and hold onto your opposite elbows, forearms, fingers, or wrists.

Keep your head on the floor whilst tucking your chin to your chest. Pull your knees to your chest as you press the back of your neck, shoulders, sacrum, and tailbone to the floor.

Relax your feet, hips, and legs. Press your belly into your thighs as you inhale. Exhale and relax all your limbs to the ground so you are lying flat again.

SUPINE BOUND ANGLE
Avoid if you have a hip and/or shoulder injury.

Bend your legs to bring the bottoms of your feet together. Your knees bend facing out like the bound angle pose but lying down.

Allow your knees to drop to the ground. You can rest your hands on your thighs to "encourage" them. Do not push them down.

As you inhale slide your arms on the ground over your head until your palms are together. Cross your thumbs.

Exhale as you return to a lying position.

CORPSE POSE

Lie flat on your back on the floor. You can place a pillow under your head if you want. Keep your head straight, i.e., don't let it fall to the side.

Draw your shoulder blades down and open your chest towards your chin.

Have your arms at a comfortable distance from your body with your palms facing up. Completely relax your arms and fingers.

Lift and extend your buttocks to your heels so that your whole sacrum rests on the floor. Keep your abdomen soft and relaxed.

Stretch your legs out straight one at the time. Allow them to roll out to the side from the hips to the feet. Check that your body is in a straight line and you are resting evenly on the left and right sides.

Once you are comfortable stay still and quiet. Be aware of your body relaxing deeper into the floor.

Allow your eyes to rest completely so they sink deeper towards the back of the skull. Relax your whole face and body.

Be aware of your breath, quiet and soft.

Now is the perfect time to do yoga nidra or some other meditation.

Yoga Cool-Down and Stretch Routine Quick-List

Transitional poses are those with *asterisks.

1. Mountain
2. Standing backbend
3. Crescent moon
4. Standing forward fold
5. Table
6. Threading the needle left
7. *Table
8. Threading the needle right
9. *Table
10. Upward dog
11. Downward dog
12. *Table
13. Low warrior left
14. Half prayer twist left
15. Half pyramid left
16. *Table
17. Low warrior right
18. Half prayer twist right
19. Half pyramid right
20. *Table
21. Extended dog
22. *Table
23. Hero
24. Lion
25. Downward frog
26. Staff
27. Seated forward bend
28. *Staff
29. Bound angle
30. *Staff
31. Seated angle
32. Side seated angle left
33. *Seated angle
34. Side seated angle right
35. *Seated angle
36. *Staff
37. Joyful baby
38. Wind relieving
39. Supine bound angle
40. Corpse

YOGA NIDRA

Yoga Nidra is a form of guided meditation which has many health benefits. You can guide yourself but the easiest way to do it is to listen to a Yoga Nidra practice and do what the instructor says.

In the Survival Fitness Plan it is recommended to do **AT LEAST** ten minutes of Yoga Nidra immediately following the yoga cool-down.

Yoga Nidra is used in the Survival Fitness Plan because it is guided meditation which makes it relatively easy to do, especially for beginners to meditation. For those of you that use other forms of mediation that you enjoy then feel free to stick to them. The main thing is that you do some sort meditation.

For best results find a place where your body can be comfortable and you can practice undisturbed. Not too hot or cold. Put on some soothing background music if you want.

It is best not to do Yoga Nidra in bed because you will be more likely to fall asleep. A yoga mat on the floor is ideal.

Yoga Nidra is a conscious practice.

Note: 10 minutes is very short for Yoga Nidra. If you can spare the extra time you can download some really good Yoga Nidra practices for free at:

YogaNidraNetwork.org/downloads.

Lie in Corpse Pose

Lie in corpse posed as previously explained.

Corpse pose, a.k.a. Shavasana, is a yoga pose used at the end of almost every yoga practice. Going straight from your yoga practice to Yoga Nidra is ideal and is (in my opinion) most likely the intention of the ones who created it.

Yoga Nidra can also be done from a sitting position if lying down is inappropriate.

Close your eyes.

Notice Your Breath

Notice your breathing. Feel your lungs filling with air, your stomach expanding, and then deflating.

Imagine a light around your body expanding and contracting as you breathe in and out.

Feel the energy coursing through your body.

Use Your Senses

Notice each of your senses individually.

What sounds do you hear? Near, far, inside, outside.

What smells can you smell? Take small sniffs, like a dog does.

Taste the air.

Feel your body supported on the floor. Which parts of your body are touching?

What can you see with your eyes closed? Does the light make shapes in your eyelids?

Repeat Your Mantra

Your mantra is a short sentence stating your intentions. It's kind of like an affirmation. It may be an overall statement of health, relaxation, etc., or may be a visualization of something you want to achieve.

Whatever it is repeat it mentally three times. Try to feel how it feels as if the visualization was realized.

One I use often is "My entire being is completely relaxed and at one with the universe."

Scan Your Body

This is where you consciously relax each part of your body.

Mentally go through your body. Bring your attention to and relax each part. You can be very detailed about this or just do large areas.

I start from the top of my head and work my way down. Sometimes I even do internal organs.

After you have relaxed smaller body parts relax them as a whole, e.g., shoulder, upper arm, bicep, elbow, forearm, hand, fingers, relax the whole arm.

At the end relax the whole body as one.

Awaken the Body

The last step is to slowly deepen your breath and start to move your fingers and toes, then your hands and feet.

In your own time stretch your body out however feels right. Open your eyes when you are ready.

When you are done stretching gently hug your knees (wind relieving pose). Fall to your right side and then gently sit up.

Take a moment to reflect on the practice and then go about your day.

ESSENTIAL PARKOUR TRAINING

INTRODUCTION

Parkour is one of the most useful skills for getting out of immediate danger when on land.

This training manual focuses on "essential" parkour movements.

By essential I mean those movements and techniques which, with basic training, would be relatively safe to use "on a whim", i.e., if you are running away from someone in an unfamiliar area.

Why Learn Parkour?

The main reason for learning parkour is for the same reason it was invented in the first place, i.e., to develop the ability to get from one point to another as efficiently as possible. There are other benefits also such as:

- It is a fun and challenging way to keep fit. It's exercising without feeling like you are exercising. You just learn the skills and physical fitness is a welcomed by-product.
- Socializing with other parkour enthusiasts. Or if you prefer to be a loner, parkour can be practiced solo.
- Seeing the world around you in a new light. Once you start to learn parkour you will no longer see buildings, stairs, rails, or any other structure in the same way again.
- Overcoming fear and building confidence. Many parkour movements, e.g., jumping gaps, can be daunting. Just like overcoming any fear, you will be able to use this inner strength in other areas of life.
- Increasing your imagination. Figuring out different ways to get from point to point using different parkour skills.

Progression

Proper progression in parkour is useful for breaking through fear as well as for safety.

Conquer small milestones and gradually increase to bigger goals. Once you successfully complete something once it will get easier. On the flip side, do not get too cocky. That is how injuries occur.

In this book the techniques are given in a progressive manner according to the type of movement (landing, vault, wall, etc.) but it does not mean you need to learn all (or any) of one type of movement before starting to train in another. Any type of movement can be practiced at your discretion.

There is one exception:

Proper landing techniques should be learned first to prevent injury. In particular, the safety tap and safety rolling.

Also, the way in which each technique is presented uses progressive steps.

Techniques are presented using the method taught in the Survival Fitness Plan but there are many ways to learn the same thing. If something doesn't work for you try a different way. Adopt the philosophy of using what is good for you and discarding what is not.

Although parkour can be practiced solo, for most people, having a training partner helps with progression since you will learn from and motivate each-other. It is also good for safety.

Training for Reality

Awareness

Constantly be aware of your surroundings. Use your peripheral vision and formulate a plan of escape when-ever you enter a new situation (notice where the exits are, how you would overcome obstacles, etc.).

A side effect of this is that being aware is transparent. People (would be attackers) notice that you are aware which makes you less of a target.

Outdoors

Train in all terrains, in all types of weather, and in all different types of light.

There are some exceptions, for example, I would not attempt some of the parkour movements on slippery surfaces.

If something is too dangerous to do during training, then it is also too dangerous to do in real life. Remember this for if you ever have to make the decision about what to do.

It is also important to vary your training grounds.

Training in the same place all the time will limit your imagination and different situations will require different skills.

Parkour and Self-Defense

It is highly recommended to combine your parkour training with self-defense. They complement each-other very well, e.g., tic-tac to side kick.

Learn more about Self Defense training at:

www.SurvivalFitnessPlan.com/Self-Defense-Training

Training on Both Sides

In reality you should favor the strong side of your body when doing actions.

When training, do so on both sides so if you cannot use your strong side (e.g., injury) then even your weaker side is still pretty good.

What You Carry

If you habitually carry a bag and are not willing to leave it behind when threatened, then you should train with it on. The tighter fitting the bag is to your body the less it will move around when training.

What You Wear

If what you wear in training is not the same thing you wear most of the time, then you will not know if you can perform the actions in everyday life. For example, how often do you go out with your climbing shoes on and chalk in your back pocket? If the answer is always then feel free to use climbing shoes and chalk when training in the Survival Fitness Plan.

Q. So I should train in my suit and tie or skirt and high heels?
A. Yes and no.

Training in clothing that is impracticable for physical exercise will only hinder your progress, but you should do it at least once in a while so you know the differences when performing actions in that type of clothing.

You may also want to consider changing what you do wear day to day to ensure functionality in movement. Loose fitting clothing and sensible shoes can be adapted to almost any situation. Before you put something on ask yourself,

"If I really need to, would I be able to sprint and climb a wall in this?"

SAFETY

Parkour is not a dangerous activity if you progress slowly, do not take unnecessary risks, and learn the correct safety techniques.

SAFETY TAP

By using the safety tap you cushion your landing which helps to prevent injuries.

It is good for those times when rolling may not be possible, e.g., lack of room, although it is best to use rolls when dropping from greater heights and/or on angles.

To do the safety tap drop down from a ledge. Start with small drops and work your way up as your confidence builds.

Land on the balls of your feet, both feet at the same time, and then roll your heels down towards the ground.

Bend your knees as you land to absorb the shock. Depending on the impact you can go all the way into a crouch.

Don't slam your wrists down. They are used for assistance and/or balance but should not be sustaining any major impact.

Spring back up using the momentum to continue your run.

Try to land as softly and quietly as possible. This is true with most things in parkour. The quieter you are the softer you are which means you put less pressure on your joints. Also, since the practical use for parkour is to run from your enemy it is advantageous to be as silent as possible.

When dropping down from a wall (e.g., from a cat hang) it is a good idea to turn away from the obstacle. You may have to use your feet to push away from the wall a little so you can get the room to turn.

SAFETY ROLLS

The safety roll is an extremely important parkour skill to develop. It is used to prevent injury from a technique gone wrong, a big drop, a general fall or trip, and/or if someone throws/pushes you to the ground or off something. It is also a good technique for transitioning between movements.

Your aim should be to make your safety roll instinctive. This is because the times you will need it most are those when you are not ready.

The safety roll can be done forwards, sideways, or backwards. You will probably use the forward roll most often but you should practice all of them regularly.

When first learning the safety roll do so on soft ground such as on grass, mats, or sand. Take it slow and start low. Once you have the technique you can progress by increasing height and/or momentum.

Forward Roll

Choose which side you are most comfortable rolling over, right or left. Eventually you want to learn to roll on both sides.

If rolling over your right shoulder start from a kneeling position with your right foot forward.

Place your hands on the ground in front of you so that your thumbs and index fingers form a kind of diamond shape. Put them at a 45° angle in the direction that you want to roll in.

Note: You could just roll over your shoulder but unless you have something in your hands it is preferable to use them to help control your motion as well as absorbing some of the impact.

Look over your left shoulder and use your rear leg to push you over into the roll. Use your hands to control your momentum and your arms to lift you a little so that you can land on the back of your shoulder blade. You do not want to hit on the top of your shoulder.

Roll diagonally across your back to your opposite hip. If you roll wrong (which you probably will when first learning) you will feel it. When you start practicing on hard surfaces you will definitely know if you are rolling poorly. It is a learning curve.

Come up from your roll between your tail and hip bones and use the side of your leg and your momentum to get back onto your feet.

You could also come straight up onto your feet as opposed to using your thigh. This saves your knee contacting the with the ground but puts more pressure on your ankle as you stand.

As you get more confident start from taller positions such as squatting and standing.

A good exercise is to stand straight and let your body fall forward like a plank.

At the last moment roll out of it. This can be done with side and back rolls also.

Also progress to rolling with momentum and with jumps.

When jumping into the roll be sure to keep your legs flexed as you land and allow the momentum to push you into the roll.

Eventually you will be able to jump and roll from ledges. It is important to slowly work your way up and increase the strength in your legs to be able to do bigger and bigger drops.

As height and speed increases it will help to land with your feet closer together and to be more adaptable with your arms.

Note: Dropping into a roll is not the same as a dive roll. When dropping from height your feet still make contact first.

Side Roll

The side roll is good for preventing injury when falling in a weird direction.

The technique is very similar to that of a forward roll except that you will roll on a more horizontal angle across your back. The exact rolling path will also depend on the angle you are falling at.

As you fall use your hands to help control your movement. Ensure you clear your arm/shoulder and land somewhere on your back.

Use the momentum to create as smooth a roll as possible and then come back onto your feet.

Back Roll

When first learning the back roll it helps to do the forward roll first. Do the forward roll and stop before getting to your feet, then roll back using the same line as you rolled forward on.

Roll forward and back a few times to get the feeling.

When ready you can back roll and come up to stand. At the end of your back roll continue to go over your shoulder.

Use your hands to push yourself up a little so you can get onto your feet.

When back rolling from a drop always try to get absorb the landing with your legs as much as possible.

Landing with one foot in behind the other will make going into the roll much easier.

Lower yourself down as much as possible and then go into the roll.

Get back to your feet as previously described.

It is important to practice rolling until it is an instinctive reaction and then to continue to practice them regularly with all variations (jumping, momentum, both sides of the body, landing at different angles, etc.).

BREAK-FALLING

Break-falling is primarily a martial arts technique used to lessen the impact when you fall. It is not very conducive to parkour because it disrupts "flow", i.e., once you break-fall you stop, but is necessary to learn for safety reasons.

Break-falling works by spreading the impact of the fall across a larger portion of your body. It may still hurt a little but much less damage will be done.

Rolling is always preferable to break-falling since it is also a swift way to get back on your feet, however, there will be times when the safety roll is not feasible, e.g., lack of space. This is when the break-fall comes in very handy.

There are a few different ways to break-fall. In the Survival Fitness Plan the Judo method is used because Judo is a martial art which makes heavy use of throwing people to the ground, hence, they really need to know how to break-fall well.

Note: After any break-fall you can return to your feet with the safety roll, or just use your hands to help you stand.

Practice break-falling on soft ground such as grass, gym mats, Sand, etc. It will also help to breathe out as you hit the ground.

For all break-falls there are two big things to watch out for.

1. Do not stick your hand down. For many people this is a natural reaction when falling but doing it will focus the impact of the fall onto a single point which is likely to cause injury.
2. Protect your head from hitting the ground. This is done differently depending on the break-fall but the basic idea is to move your head or face away from the ground.

Back Break-Fall

Stand with your feet about shoulder width apart.

Squat down as low as you can and tuck your chin to your chest.
Tucking your chin will prevent you hitting the back of your head on
the ground.

Fall onto your back and arms allowing a slight roll, but don't roll back
too much.

If you stop the roll 'dead' it will put too much pressure on your body,
but you don't want your legs to go too far towards your head for the
same reason.

Having your feet turned out a little and your knees slightly bent will
help you to control this.

Your arms splay out at about 45°.

Side Break-Fall

From a standing position step forward with your right leg and do a single leg squat as you bring your left leg through.

The more you bend the leg the closer you will be to the ground before landing.

Get as low to the ground as you can, tuck your chin to your chest, and then fall onto the left side of your torso/back and on the whole of your left arm at about 45° to your body, palm facing down.

Your legs will probably go in the air.

Allow your legs to come back to the ground finishing in a comfortable position, but not splayed too wide or crossed.

Forward Break-Fall

With the front break-fall you fall directly forward and land on your forearms.

Start on your knees so you are low to the ground. Put your arms in front of your face in an upside-down V.

As you fall towards the ground tense your core and take the impact on your forearms. Try not to let your belly hit the ground.

If you can it is a good idea to turn your face to the side (not pictured).

Once you are confident do it from a standing position. Spread your legs so you can be lower to the ground.

Eventually you can do it from full standing and also with a little jump.

Forward Roll Break-Fall

The forward roll break-fall is useful to know in case you go to roll but then there is an obstacle ahead preventing you from standing up.

Do a forward safety roll as normal but instead of coming onto your feet you stop in the side break-fall position.

From there you can do a backwards safety roll to get back to your feet.

For all break-falls, once you are confident with your technique you can try with less and less squat. Also try with different scenarios, e.g., falling off a chair.

WARM-UPS AND CONDITIONING

Use warm-ups exercises to prepare your body for vigorous activity. A proper warm up is essential to prevent injury.

Conditioning with strengthen your muscles and improve endurance.

Most of the exercises in this section are both warm-up and conditioning rolled into one.

They are all also useful as parkour movements in their own right as well as being "stepping stones" for more advanced parkour techniques in this manual.

CATWALK

The catwalk is a form of quadrupedal movement. Quadrupedal movement is the act of moving on all-fours. Other types of quadrupedal movement described in this book include side sapiens and ground kongs.

All types of quadrupedal movement have their practical use and they also make great warm-up/conditioning exercises.

The catwalk is useful when having to traverse across ledges, rails, etc., as well as to get through or under small areas. It gives you more balance and control on the obstacle and also lowers your profile which makes it great for escape and evasion.

Start by getting down on your hands (flat palms) and feet with your right hand in front of your left hand, and your left foot in front of your right foot. Your hands and feet form a line and as you move forward you want to maintain this line as close as possible. When first starting it will help to follow an actual line on the ground. When you are on a ledge or rail you will have little choice anyway.

To move forward first move your rear hand to the front, then your rear foot to the front. Repeat this. Start slowly with small steps and ensure transfer the weight evenly between your arm and legs — front and back, left and right.

For stability, keep three points of contact on the surface at all times.

Once you have gained the co-ordination of movement concentrate on perfecting your posture. Make yourself as level as possible from your hips to your head.

Keep your back flat and horizontal to the ground, and your head forward.

Don't stretch yourself out, bring your knees too close to your body, or stick your bum out.

When you need a rest, crouch. Do not put your knees on the ground.

Progress further and work different muscles by cat walking backwards, up and down stairs, getting really low, on ledges, on rails, etc.

BALANCE

The exercises that follow are used for improvement of balance which is extremely important in parkour.

They also have other advantages such as:

- Building resilient joints to help sustain the stresses of high-impact jumping and landing.
- Cultivating body awareness.
- Improving all over body strength.
- Increasing your focus levels.

Ideally you will want to be able to do all these exercises on a round rail since it is (in most places) the hardest, common, urban structure to balance on. Progress to this by starting on the ground, then on ledges, flat planks, square rails, etc.

Squatting

First you need to be able to get into the squat position on the ground.

If you do not have the flexibility for this, then the yoga stretches from Daily Health and Fitness can help. In particular, the Seated Forward Bend and Downward Dog.

Once you can do a squat on the ground, do it on the rail.

To begin with you can hold onto it.

Then once you have found your balance/confidence, let go.

It may help to focus your gaze on a single point in front of you.

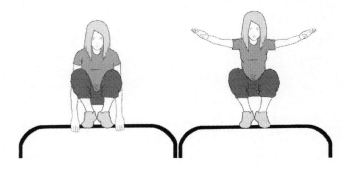

Standing

When you are ready try standing on the rail for as long as you can.

Squats

Doing squats on the rail is a great strength building exercise.

Make sure you can do at least ten squats on the ground before trying them on the rail.

Even better is to do jumping squats which combines the squat with the box jump. When you are confident you can use the box jump to get up onto the rail.

The jumping squat is detailed in the Body Conditioning chapter of Daily Health and Fitness.

Walking

The next step is to walk. Walk forward a bit, then turn around and walk back.

It will help to start on something easier than a rail. At the most basic level you can just follow a line on the ground, then use a wide plank and get thinner as you progress.

The key to keeping balance is correct posture. As you walk keep your chest up, knees slightly bent, and your bum over your heels. Take each step toes first.

Go slowly to begin with, use "airplane arms" until you are confident, and stop to regain balance when needed.

Try walking backwards also.

Note: In a real-life scenario you would most likely use a money traverse or catwalk on the rail as these two methods will give you more control and a lower profile.

Rail Balance Routine

Once you can do all the above things you can put them into a short rail balancing routine that you can do regularly.

Jump up on to the rail, get balanced in the squat position, do a few squats on the rail, stand, walk forward, turn around, walk backwards, catwalk.

Increase difficulty with inclined rails.

Slacklining

When you want to become a beast of balance you can move from the rail to slack lining. Just do the rail balancing routing on the slack-line.

Slacklining is basically tightrope walking but most people will use a dynamic (stretchy), flat, broad (a few inches) piece of webbing tied between two anchor points, usually trees.

To learn more about slackening including the various types and how to set one up visit:

Slackline.hivefly.com/slacklining-for-beginners-step-by-step

SIDE SAPIENS

Side Sapiens (a.k.a. side monkey's) are a type of quadrupedal movement which are used as a progression to the reverse vault.

They are also practical in their own right to displace momentum (such as when landing from a drop) and/or to continue flow into your next movement.

Start in a low squat position.

Reach your arms out across your body to your left and plant them firmly on the ground. Your right-hand lands first closely followed by your left.

Keep your arms strong and use them to support your body weight as you bring your legs to your left. Your right foot lands first closely followed by your left so that you are back in the low squat position.

Engage your core and land with control. Land lightly with your feet and as quietly as you can.

Repeat this movement a few times and then go back the other way.

This is also good to practice on ledges and rails.

For more of a challenge you can do this exercise with straight legs.

GROUND KONGS

Ground Kongs are a type of quadrupedal movement used as a progression to the kong vault.

They are also practical in their own right to displace momentum (such as when landing from a drop) and/or to continue flow into your next movement.

Start in a low squat position.

Reach forward and plant both your hands firmly on the ground.

Keep your arms strong and use them to support your body weight as you bring your legs up to your hands (or as close as you can).

Engage your core and land with control. Land lightly with your feet and as quietly as you can.

Repeat this movement a few times.

When you are confident practice on ledges and rails.

As you build strength you can try to cover more ground.

You can also do ground kongs backwards which will target a different set of muscles.

RUNNING AND JUMPING

This section contains techniques to do with running and jumping over or between obstacles without contacting them.

It also includes explanations of parkour runs and games.

SPRINTING

In parkour, between overcoming obstacles, you sprint.

Sprinting is also an efficient form of exercise. It is far more effective to do multiple short sprints than it is to run/jog long distance. Sprinting gives the same health benefits in a much shorter time, as well as other benefits that jogging or running do not offer.

Unlike jogging or running, when you sprint you will be creating explosive power which is very important in parkour.

Also, sprinting is very functional and much more useful than long distance jogging when it comes to escaping from danger.

If for some reason you do need to run for a long distance, then by practicing parkour in general you will have the endurance to do so — more than you would than if you just went jogging every day.

Proper Running Technique

Using proper running technique will enable you to go faster and longer whilst expending less energy.

When running (sprinting) keep your elbows bent at 90° and move your hand from your pocket to your chin.

Move your knees and elbows in unison. As you drive your elbows back, bring your knees up. Then as your hand goes to your chin, drive your leg back down.

Be sure to bring your hand from your pocket to your chin. The further back your elbows go the higher your knees will go.

Keep your chin level, eyes focused forward, core engaged, shoulders relaxed, and your torso upright (opposed to leaning forward).

This posture keeps your mass vertical which means your feet will strike the ground with more force and hence you will produce more speed.

Even when you get tired, always keep correct running form.

Breathing

While running you use up a lot of oxygen which you need to replace efficiently.

Breathe Through your Mouth

This allows more oxygen to enter your body. It also prevents you from clenching your teeth together which may cause headaches.

Note: When breathing normally, or if you have to run in high pollution, it is better to breathe through your nose. Your nose is the body's air treatment system. It filters, humidifies, and warms the air before it reaches the rest of your body.

Use Belly Breathing

Learn this first by lying on your back. As you exhale use your stomach muscles to help expel all the air out of your lungs. To inhale just relax your stomach muscles and let the air come in.

Once you are comfortable with belly breathing use it while sprinting.

Breathe in Step

Breathing in time to your steps is the easiest way to regulate the rhythm of your breath. This is useful to monitor and control certain things while you are running.

At a normal run rate (not sprinting) stay at a 2:2 ratio. This means to inhale over two steps and then exhale over two steps.

During harder runs you may need to change the ratio to 1:2 or 2:1.

When you go up a hill maintain the same ratio of breath as you were using before the hill. This ensures you use the same amount of energy to get over the hill.

To fix a side-stitch while running slow your breathing to a deeper 3:3 rhythm.

Another way to fix a stitch is to expand and contract your diaphragm in the opposite direction as normal. When you breathe in make your stomach contract, and when you exhale make your stomach expand.

Note: Breathing at a 1:1 ratio or faster may lead to hyperventilation, and if using a 3:3 ratio or slower you may not get enough oxygen into your body.

EVASIVE RUNNING

Evasive Running is the ability to maneuver out of the way of an oncoming or stationary obstacle whilst running.

When learning evasive running use a running speed slightly slower than sprinting. You want to be quick but not so quick that you will get injured whilst performing the movement.

Train to evade humans as they will be the hardest in terms of "out smarting" them. You want to go in whichever direction is hardest for your opponent to go.

As you approach your opponent look him in the eye. It will make it harder for him to predict where you are going and he will probably think you are charging straight at him.

If your opponent is square on with you but is not on the balls of his feet, i.e., flat footed (left picture) then it should be fairly easy to pass him on either side.

If he has one side forward more, evade him by going to the other side of his body. It will probably be his weaker side and will also be harder for him to maneuver in that direction. In the right picture you would maneuver to her left since her right foot is forward.

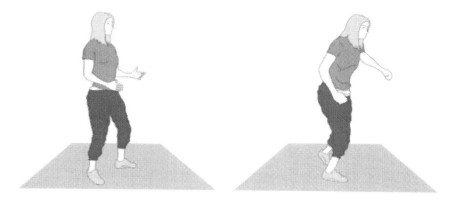

If he angles away from you then go the opposite way. In the picture she has stepped to her left with her right foot. Evade to her right, to the outside of her.

You can practice this with a friend. Have your friend face you square on as you run towards him. When you are close your friend steps toward you and you evade in the best direction.

You could also practice against a stationary object. Run towards it and evade on either side at the last moment.

HURDLES

Hurdles are often neglected in parkour but they are the fastest way to pass an obstacle, and sometimes the only way, i.e., when you cannot touch it (chain link fences, hedges, etc.)

Since hurdles are the most efficient way to pass an obstacle you should use them whenever possible. They are best used over small obstacles that you are confident you can clear.

The mechanics of the hurdle can be learned with a couple of drills.

Trail Leg Drill

The trail leg drill teaches you to lift your rear leg up and to the outside as opposed to coming straight through.

Face a wall just over one natural step away and lean your palms flat against it. Bring your left leg straight up behind you and then bring your knee to the front coming out to the side, i.e., parallel to your hip.

Keep your heel directly behind your knee far as you can and then snap your foot back down to the ground.

Do this drill ten times on each side of your body.

Front Leg Drill

The front leg drill teaches you to lean forward which is very important for momentum.

Stand facing a wall just over one natural step away from it.

Thrust your front leg straight up and into the wall. Really lean into it. As you bring your leg up reach forward with your opposite hand.

Do this drill ten times on each side of your body.

The Hurdle

After you have practiced those two drills you can try the actual hurdle.

Approach the obstacle with enough speed so that you are confident you will clear it.

Thrust your lead foot and opposite arm forward as you kick your rear leg straight back.

As your body comes over the obstacle bring your rear knee to the front, parallel to your hip.

Land on your lead foot and continue running forward.

PRECISION JUMPING

Precision jumping is a fundamental parkour skill in which you jump from one stationary point to another. It is important to learn how to be precise with your landings so you can land safely on smaller obstacles such as ledges, hand rails, and walls.

When doing precision jumping your aim is to land exactly on your intended landing spot with no extra momentum in either direction, e.g., without stumbling forward.

Begin with your feet together and bend your knees a little so you are in a semi-crouch position.

Move your arms behind you as you shift your weight to the balls of your feet.

Lean forward. The greater the distance you need to jump, the more you need to lean.

As you jump throw your arms forwards and upwards.

Your energy travels up the legs, through the torso, and into the hands.

Aim to arc up and then come down on to the landing area, landing on the balls of your feet as quiet as you can. Land on both feet at the same time, similar to the safety tap.

As you build confidence start jumping from farther back and with small level differences, such as onto a curb.

You can also try high to low, to/from rails, etc.

Note: When jumping onto smaller platforms (such as handrails) it is extra important that you aim to land on the balls of your feet. This way if you slip a little then you have the whole of your foot to recover. If you land on your heels and slip you will probably fall.

Jumping Larger Gaps

Note: It is a good idea to learn the crane landing before attempting larger gaps just in case you jump short.

Practice precision jumping over larger gaps on the ground first to see if you can make it. This is also useful to improve your distance.

Use lines on the road or any other type of marker so you can take off and land on exact points.

When doing longer precision jumps focus more on extending your body out.

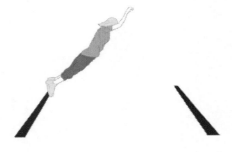

Once you are in the air bring your knees forward.

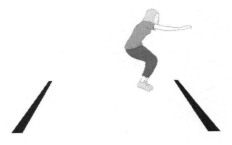

Push your feet towards the landing point.

Land as softly as you can.

Running Precision Jumps

When precision jumping over very large gaps you can use the running precision jump. The running precision jump is exactly what it sounds like, i.e., a precision jump with a run up, as opposed to leaping from a stationary position.

The running precision jump uses a one foot take off. You still land in the same way as a standing precision jump, i.e., a precise double foot landing.

Since you are jumping with much more momentum "sticking" the landing becomes more difficult and many people find they jump too far and/or stumble forward when landing.

CRANE LANDING

The crane landing is used when you want to land on obstacles that are just a bit too far (either in height or distance) to precision jump onto but still small enough that you do not feel the need to cat hang or vault.

Your intention is to have one of your feet land on top of the obstacle while the other one supports you down the front of it.

Prepare to jump just like a precision jump.

Making the decision of whether you would make the precision jump may be done either before you jump or mid-air.

Put the foot that you intend to land on top of the obstacle with in front.

Your front foot lands on top while your rear foot pushes against the front of the obstacle to prevent you from falling back.

Once you are stable bring your rear foot up onto the obstacle.

STRIDING

Parkour striding, a.k.a., bounding, is leaping from one foot to another in succession. It is useful for running across elevated obstacles.

Approach the stride like a running precision. Run up and take off from one foot.

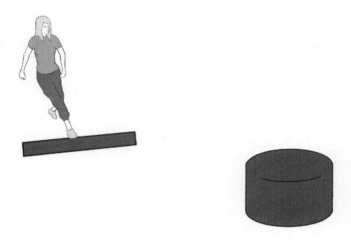

Elongate and stretch your legs out front and back.

As your lead leg lands you want your center of gravity to be over your foot so you can push off into the next stride. If you are too far forward or back it will mess up your momentum.

It will help to get your arms and leg in sync, just as if you were walking, i.e., whichever foot is in front the opposite arm is also in front.

You can use this arm swing to generate more power. The further the distance between your obstacles the more you should swing your arms.

STRIDE TO SAFETY STEP

The stride to safety step is used to stride over a gap onto a ledge (or similar) and then safely move down a level, such as to the ground. It is actually a combination of two other parkour techniques, i.e., striding and the safety step-through (a.k.a. down step).

Note: Before you attempt the stride to safety step you should know how to stride and how to do the safety vault (the safety step through is covered as part of the safety vault).

Run up to the first ledge and stride off it as normal.

Land on the second ledge one foot first. Most people find it easiest to land on the opposite foot they took off with but either foot is possible.

As you land lean out a little to the opposite side of the foot you landed on. This is so you have enough room for your other leg to come through.

Allow your leg to absorb most of the impact and then place your hand on the ledge, fingers pointing out to your side.

Your other leg comes through between your hand and foot so you can push yourself away from the edge.

Here is a view from the front.

This demonstrated leaving off one leg and then landing on the opposite one, which is the way most people prefer to do it.

You could also leave off one leg and then land on the same one. Experiment to see which you prefer.

It also showed going from lower to higher, but you can do it between surfaces of the same level, or from higher to lower.

DIVE ROLL

The dive roll is used to prevent injury when coming down on your head.

In most cases this is intentional in the way of diving over an obstacle, but may also used in accidental falls where you are low to the ground and don't have the room to land feet first, e.g., your foot clips on the obstacle while hurdling.

Note: In the case that you fell (or were thrown) off something high then, if possible, landing feet first and doing a safety roll is your best option.

Ensure you are proficient at the safety roll before attempting the dive roll.

Avoid doing the dive roll on hard ground, even when proficient.

The technique for doing the dive roll is very similar to the forward roll but there is a lot more impact and momentum. Also, you are coming doing toward your head as opposed to landing on your feet first.

Start by practicing the forward roll from a handstand. You don't need to be great at handstands, you just have to get at the right angle for a moment so you can go into the roll.

Lower yourself with your arms then lean forward slightly to tuck your head as you go into the roll.

Keep your body strong (arms, core, legs, and neck) as you allow your body to "collapse" into the roll.

Once you are comfortable you can start jumping into the dive roll from a standing position.

Kick your leg back as you jump to help get your hips over.

As you hit the ground absorb some of the impact with your arms by keeping them strong whilst allowing them to collapse. Also use your arms to ensure you get over your head.

Use the momentum to flow onto your back and into the roll.

Next try it with a short run up, and then try jumping off with two feet.

Slowly progress until you are doing a full dive roll.

Dive and stretch out like a cat.

Absorb the impact with your arms.

Tuck your head as you go into the roll.

Train at this level until you have it instinctive, then progress by jumping higher and over things.

When jumping over things ensure your hips clear the obstacle and your legs/feet follow in the same path.

PARKOUR RUNS

A parkour run is when you put your parkour skills into practical use. Basically the idea is to go from one point to another in the most efficient manner. All you need is a few basic techniques and you can start.

To begin with you may just want to do a "short run" with two or three techniques put together in a flow. You can "suss out" a site first so you know exactly what you want to do.

Try different things to see what works best (fastest and most efficient) for you. Practice each technique individually and then put them together. Gradually get faster and faster.

Eventually you want to be able to go from point A to point B long distance without having to suss it out first, i.e., just overcoming obstacles as you come to them.

Good runs are those when the transition between techniques is smooth. Once confident your aim should be to move as quickly and quietly as possible, adapting to your environment as you go.

PARKOUR GAMES

Parkour games are a good way to vary your training. They are great for kids and adults alike. There are many types of parkour games. Most of them are just adaptations of games you probably already know. Here are a couple of examples.

Horse

One person does a technique or short run and the others have to replicate it. If they are unable to replicate it, they get a letter "H".

Once they have used up all their letters (HORSE) they are out of the game. Take turns being the person that does the technique that the others have to replicate.

Of course the word you spell can be anything, e.g., PARKOUR.

Quadrupedal Tag

Play a game of tag but you are only allowed to use different types of quadrupedal movement (ground kongs, side sapiens, cat walking, etc.).

This concept can easily be applied to many games such as capture the flag.

You could also just play normal tag but now you get to use your parkour skills.

Lava Pit

A childhood favorite where you pretend the ground is molten lava. Move around being sure not to fall in. This is easily combined with tag also.

VAULTS

Technically a vault is any type of movement that involves overcoming an obstacle, but in this section it only refers to those movements in which you make contact with the obstacle you are going over.

SAFETY VAULT

The safety vault is used to pass a relatively low and short obstacle in front of you such as a waist-height wall.

Learning how to do the safety vault is a good first vault to learn because it is the easiest and the safest to do.

It is also a necessary technique to know so you can progress to the similar but faster speed vault, the reverse safety vault, and the stride to safety step techniques.

An easy way to learn the safety vault is by numbering your hands and feet.

It will help you to remember the order of placement.

1. Left hand.
2. Right leg.
3. Left leg.
4. Right hand.

Take it slow to begin with. Get the pattern into your head, and eventually into your muscle memory.

Approach the obstacle and place your left hand (#1) on it.

Next place your right leg (#2).

Stretch it out far enough to allow your left leg (#3) to pass though between your left hand and right leg.

Step straight through with your left leg. Keep you right arm (#4) up so you can pass your leg through easier.

Here is what it looks like from the front.

Practice on both sides of your body.

When you add speed your #1 leg doesn't have to push off that much. It becomes just a touch on top of the obstacle so you can gauge where it is.

As you run up to the obstacle be sure not to stop in preparation for the vault. Stride directly onto it and go up and over the object in an arc.

Land with your chest above or in front of your foot and use your #1 and #2 to push the object behind you so you get more forward momentum. At the same time reach with your #3 leg down to the floor.

SPEED VAULT

The speed vault is used to quickly pass over small to medium sized obstacles that are too big for you to hurdle over. Before attempting the speed vault you should be proficient at the safety vault.

Note: If you are approaching an obstacle at an angle use the lazy vault.

The speed vault is basically the same as a safety vault except you do not let your foot touch the wall. To get your legs coordinated for this you can do the following exercise.

If you want to place your left hand on the obstacle, then raise your right leg straight out to your right. Quickly follow it with your left. Tap your right foot with your left in the air.

Be sure to raise your right and then your left, as opposed to jumping with both legs at the same time. Your left foot lands back on the ground first.

This leg kicking motion is what you use to pass the obstacle, except without tapping your feet.

Approach the object with some speed so you can clear it. Like with most vaults you want to arc over the obstacle. Run and kick your legs up. Once you are in the air, place your hand on the obstacle (fingers facing forwards) and push up and back to help get your chest and legs through.

Keep your chest pointing forward and do not hold onto the wall too long otherwise it will focus your momentum in a different direction (as opposed to straight ahead).

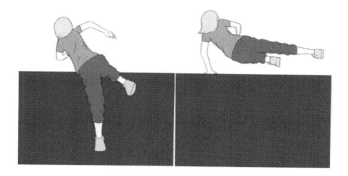

Switch your legs through while you are in the air and land on your inside foot first, i.e., the same side foot as your hand on the wall. As you land your chest should be facing forward and in front of your leading leg. Be sure to push the obstacle behind you before landing.

Note: If you want to exit on a direction other than straight ahead try to face your chest in the direction you want to go and use your hand on the wall as a pivot point.

TURN VAULT

The turn vault can be used to pass over a rail, wall, fence, ledge, etc. in a swift and safe manner. Besides passing over as usual, another common use of the turn vault is to cat hang (or just hang) over the other side of an obstacle before dropping down.

It is a good idea to learn the safety vault before attempting the turn vault. This will give you a basic understanding of the body mechanics need to get over an obstacle and also helps to build confidence.

When first learning the turn vault do it over a rail as opposed to a wall. Also, if you are worried about clearing the height you can first try it at the end of the rail so your legs can just come around the end if needed.

Start with a rail about waist height.

Place your hands on the rail a comfortable width apart (shoulder width is usually good) one hand faced up and the other faced down.

Whichever hand faces down is the direction your legs will go. It is also the hand you will take off the rail.

Squat back so your arms are almost straight and then push up with your legs while pulling with your arms to arc up and over the rail. Your legs circle around to the side.

Your chest comes over the bar first. As your legs come over the bar release your hand so you can complete the 180° spin.

Once you are on the other side place your hand back on the bar in an overhand position at about the same distance as it was originally.

As you are doing this you also want to be looking for where to place your feet.

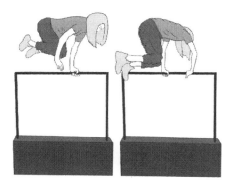

As you come down to land lean back a little and place your feet on the target. Leaning back allows the energy to get pushed through your feet which will give you a good grip.

Don't worry if you can't get your hand and foot in the right place on the other side right away. Just keep practicing.

Once you can do the turn vault on a rail smoothly you can progress to a wall/ledge. You will need to adjust your hand positioning since you can't grab under a wall. Somewhere close to 90° to the side is good.

Come over in the usual way but use less speed so you can hold yourself up on the other side.

Once you are stable you can drop down into a cat hang or do whatever else you want.

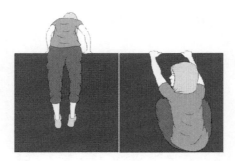

Once you are confident/have built enough strength you can use more speed and go straight into cat hang.

REVERSE SAFETY VAULT

The reverse safety vault (a.k.a. reverse step vault) is exactly what it sounds like, i.e., the safety vault in reverse.

It is a good progression technique to the reverse vault but it also has a lot of practical uses in its own right.

If you are backed up against an obstacle you can use the reverse safety vault to pass over it without having to turn to face it. Then you can either land to face your aggressor or land facing away so you can run.

You could also use it to back out of numerous types of forward facing vaults if you see danger on the other side.

Stand with your back to the obstacle and place your right hand on it, fingers facing forward.

"Hop up" onto the obstacle with your left foot making contact.

Push off with your left foot so that you turn to your left and land on the other side facing away from the obstacle. Land on your right foot first.

Eventually you want to be able to do this smoothly without having to look at your foot as you come up onto the obstacle.

Also practice it so you stay facing the same way. Instead of pushing off with your left foot to spin you just step your right foot through onto the ground.

LAZY VAULT

The lazy vault is useful when approaching a small to medium sized obstacle at an angle other than straight on, and no matter what speed your approach is.

It can be used when coming in and out on a similar angle and it can also be adapted to exit on a different angle.

Assuming you are approaching the obstacle from the right, your limbs will go over the wall in this order:

1. Right hand.
2. Right leg.
3. Left leg.
4. Left hand.

This first progression step will help you to get the mechanics of the technique.

Approach the wall on a diagonal from the right and place your right hand (#1) on the wall as you jump up. Your right leg (#2) goes through and you land on the wall with your left foot (#3).

Drop down to the ground landing on your right foot first (#2) and then continue to run.

Here it is from behind.

Once you are ready you can learn the actual lazy vault which means you will not place your left foot (#3) on the wall.

Kick your legs up over the wall and bring your hips up.

As you go over your left hand (#4) replaces your right on the obstacle.

Use your left hand to help push your hips away from the obstacle so you can continue running.

A "proper" lazy vault means that you approach on an angle and exit along the same path. Ensure your limbs go over in the right order and that you land/run out on #2.

If you want to exit on a different angle just turn your hips in the direction you want to go while in the air.

If you are exiting on a different angle unintentionally it may be because you are forgetting to put your #4 hand down.

KONG VAULT

The kong vault (also known as the cat pass, monkey vault, kong leap, etc.) is useful for vaulting longer or higher obstacles. It is a bit more difficult than previous vaults explained in this book but is worth the practice because it is extremely useful.

Start on something like a picnic table, i.e., wide enough to land on but not too high, and small enough to vault over (eventually).

This first progression exercise is helpful to get over the fear of hitting your toes on the obstacle.

Stand at one end of the obstacle and place your palms flat on it a little more than shoulder width apart with your fingers facing forwards.

Use your arms to support you as you jump up onto the obstacle, landing with your feet between your hands. Move your hands away as needed.

Repeat this exercise until you are comfortable with the mechanics.

When ready try to land further and further forward with your feet by pushing the obstacle back underneath you. The more you push the further you can go.

Next try starting with some distance between you and the obstacle.

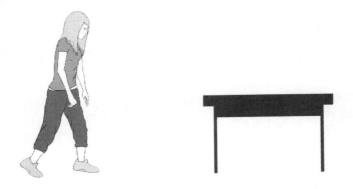

Take a one or two step "run up" then do the same as before.

Let the momentum help you to get further onto the obstacle.

To get even further you can run up with a bit more momentum using one of two take-offs depending on the type of obstacle.

First try the two-foot punch take off which most people find easier. It will redirect momentum up which makes it better for high obstacles.

Start further away from the obstacle than you have been.

Run up and hop on one foot then land on both feet together. You will need practice to learn where a good distance is for you to land back from the obstacle.

Use the momentum to go into a dive onto the obstacle then complete the vault as normal.

Next try the split foot take off. The split foot take-off has more forward momentum than the two-foot punch take off which makes it better for longer obstacles.

Start at about the same distance as you did for the two -foot punch take off.

Run up and hop on one foot then land on the opposite one. Take another quick step and then push up with both feet to go into the dive.

Complete the vault as before.

Try to get further and further until you can clear the obstacle.

To get more distance increase your approach speed and use the split foot take off.

Kick out your feet to raise your hips which will help stretch out your dive.

Spot where you want your hands to land and then push up and forward as your arms make contact.

Land on two feet to begin with and then progress into landing in a one- two motion so you can resume running.

Once you are comfortable try the kong vault on higher and/or longer obstacles using the appropriate take off, i.e., two-foot punch for higher and split foot for longer.

REVERSE VAULT

The reverse vault is useful when you have a lot of momentum but not enough space to dive or swing your leg. This may be because two obstacles are very close together, or perhaps someone as swung you with your back towards an obstacle.

There are two good ways to learn the reverse vault.

The first is to get faster and faster at the reverse safety vault. The more you do it the less you need to put the weight on the foot until eventually you will be able to get all the way over the obstacle and land on the other side, i.e., the reverse vault.

The second way is to build up from side sapiens. For detailed instructions on how to do side sapiens see the section on warm-ups and conditioning.

Once you are comfortable with side sapiens try the following twisting variation of it. Face your body forwards and then place your hands as if doing side sapiens but at a 90° angle.

Use your arms to support your weight as you turn in a circle until you are facing forward again.

This twisting motion variation of side sapiens can also be adapted to save you from a seated fall, i.e., if you are sitting on something and fall (or are pushed) backwards.

The next progression is to do side sapiens over an obstacle.

When you are ready, add a full twist as you come down out of it.

Land on your foot closest to the obstacle first and keep spinning until you are facing away from it.

Finally, start the twist from the beginning.

And finish by landing in the same way as before.

Practice this vault immediately after other vaults when the obstacles are close together and also while being flung into one.

An opponent grabs you and begins to fling you into an obstacle.

When you are about a step away from the obstacle start to turn your back to it.

Place your hand on the obstacle first to help gauge distance and direct momentum as you vault over it.

WALL TECHNIQUES

This section covers all the techniques that are predominantly associated with the wall. They are mostly to do with overcoming obstacles that are too big to vault.

CAT LEAP TO CAT HANG

The cat leap (a.k.a. the arm jump, arm leap, etc.) to cat hang is a commonly used technique in which you jump towards a vertical obstacle (cat leap) and hang off it (cat hang).

The standard cat leap is from a precision or running jump but other techniques are often used also such as a kong vault, a lache, etc.

Once in the cat hang you can choose to drop down, climb up, cat to cat, etc. The cat hang is also very useful in its own right since it can be used to lower yourself to the ground, e.g., turn vault to cat hang and then drop down.

When first learning the cat leap to cat hang start from a stationary position fairly close to the obstacle.

As you jump toward the obstacle lean back a little and bring your feet and hands out in front of you. Arc into your landing and connect with the obstacle feet first so that they can absorb the impact.

Keep a little space between your feet as you land so if you fall back you have more control.

If it is a low obstacle, avoid landing too high on it otherwise you will find it harder to grab the top.

Note: It is very important to connect with the obstacle feet first. If you don't then you will probably just slam into the obstacle.

Once you have grabbed onto the top of the obstacle you can straighten your arms so you are "crouching" against the wall. This is the cat hang. From here you can drop down or climb-up.

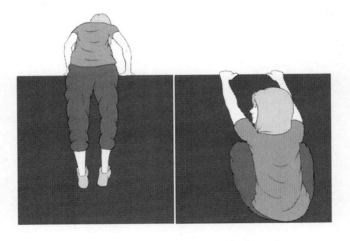

If the obstacle isn't too high, you may be able go straight into the up position of the wall climb-up.

If dropping down kick away from the obstacle a little bit and turn away from it on your way down. Land with a safety tap or roll.

Practice with different heights, distances, etc., so you get used adjusting your jump in different circumstances.

CAT TO CAT

The cat to cat is when you leap from one cat hang to another one on an opposing obstacle.

Before learning the cat to cat you need to know the cat hang.

Find two obstacles that directly face one another. This makes it easier to learn to begin with.

Go into a cat hang on the first obstacle.

Turn you head to spot where you are going to land and push off with one of your legs as you let go with your hands.

Immediately turn to face the second obstacle and reach out with your other leg (the opposite of the one you pushed off with) so it is ready to absorb the impact before taking grip with your hands to land in a cat hang.

Once confident practice with different angles, heights, cat to precision, cat to crane, cat to lache, etc.

In all cases the main thing is to be aware of is how your feet and hands hit the wall.

When going from low to high you want to get a lot of pressure into the wall so that your feet don't slip as you push your body up.

When going from high to low make sure that you still get your feet out in front of you and that you're lowering yourself into the landing with your chest back. This will prevent you hitting your face.

TIC-TAC

A tic-tac is when you push your foot off an obstacle on an angled direction. It is a fairly simple technique which can be used to help clear gaps, leap over obstacles, gain height, or for a quick redirection of your momentum.

A horizontal wall run is a progression of the tic-tac in which you take multiple steps along the wall as opposed to just one.

To begin with just get used to how the obstacle feels under your foot. Walk up to the obstacle, place your foot on it, and then push off in a slight upward manner so you arc back onto the ground. Whichever foot your push off with land on your opposite foot first and then continue to walk away.

You can either focus your tic-tac on pushing away from the obstacle or pushing along it so experiment with both by facing your chest and shoulders towards your destination.

Next start to add some momentum and try to get more and more distance and/or height.

The more momentum you have the harder you can push off the wall and the higher and/or farther you will be able to get. Also, the higher you place your foot on the obstacle the more lift and distance you will achieve.

Once you are confident you can start doing it over objects.

Concentrate on your foot placement so you can get enough leverage off the wall to clear the object.

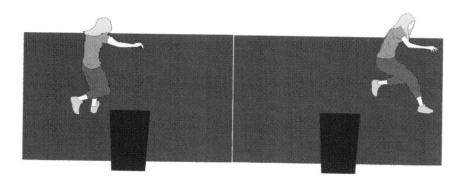

Then try with multiple steps. This is where the tic-tac turns into the horizontal wall run.

Approach at a smaller angle between you and the wall.

First try with two steps, then three or more.

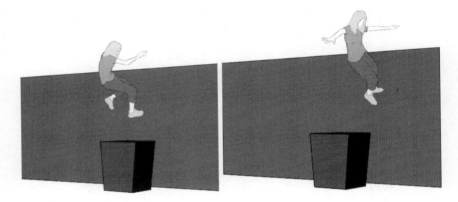

The tic-tac can also be used to help overcome higher obstacles.

WALL CLIMB-UP

The wall climb-up is used to pull yourself from a hanging position up onto a wall in a quick and efficient manner.

When first learning it will help to use the momentum from a cat leap or wall run to help get up the wall. Eventually you will want to be able to do it from a static hang.

Start on a wall you can easily cat leap to cat hang to so you can get the most out of momentum.

As soon as you have a grip on the obstacle use your feet to push your hips back as you pull up and in with your arms. Push your feet into the obstacle, not down. Try to straighten your highest leg.

Your leg push and arm pull is one smooth motion. The aim is to get your chest above the top of the obstacle.

As your chest comes over you need to transition from your hands hanging to your hands on top. For most people this is the hardest part of the climb-up.

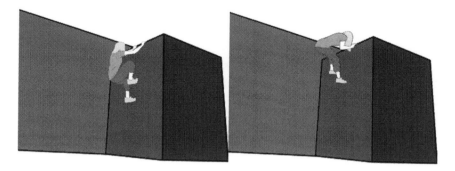

Using the momentum from the push/pull quickly take the weight off your hands and 'pop' them on top of the obstacle so that your palms are on it.

The more you can push against the obstacle and the more momentum you have the easier it will be.

Once your hands are on top, push up. Keep your chest forward so you don't fall back.

To make things a little easier you can do the transition one arm at a time and then progress to doing them together when you're ready.

To stand on the obstacle use one of your feet to kick out a little so you can bring your other foot up on top.

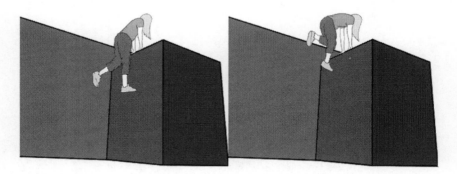

Avoid using your elbows and knees to help you.

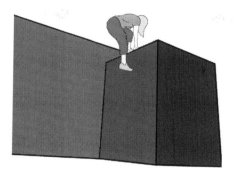

Alternatively, you can do the wall pop-up to stand.

Once you can do the wall climb-up try doing it from a static hang.

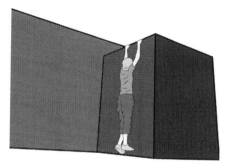

Push your body against the obstacle a little to help pop your hips back.

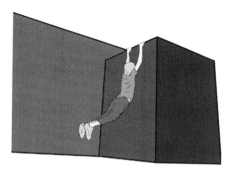

As your legs swing back in, place one foot on the wall and then get your other leg as high as possible so you can transition into the wall climb-up.

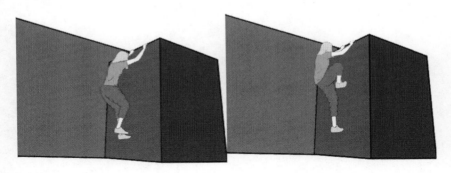

Correct technique is what will get you on top of an obstacle but having more strength will make it easier, especially when doing it from a static hang. Some useful exercises to help build strength are:

- **Dips.** With your hands in front of your chest to mimic the climb-up, as opposed to being out to your sides.
- **Pull ups.** Standard pull-ups. Not to be confused with chin-ups.
- **Reverse climb-ups.** Start from on top of the wall and slowly lower yourself down by reversing the climb-up action.
- **Super-burpees.** The ultimate all-round conditioning exercise.
- **Traversing.** Hang off an obstacle and traverse around it.

Eventually you can progress to a one-armed wall climb-up from a static hang.

VERTICAL WALL RUN

Use the vertical wall run to get up tall obstacles.

To practice the vertical wall run you can use any obstacle that is tall enough. You don't have to be able to reach the top to practice but if you can it means you can also practice your wall climb (or other techniques) at the same time. Small wall runs may also be used as part of a wall pop-up.

Initially you will have to get familiar with your steps so you have the right spacing when approaching the obstacle. After a while this becomes intuitive.

Find a spot where you are comfortable with your leg resting on the obstacle at about hip height. Not too close where you're pushing in and not too far away where you are stretching to reach.

Once you have found that space you can start to get comfortable with stepping a foot onto the obstacle and jumping off it. Don't worry about gaining height yet.

Use your strong leg against the obstacle first as that is the one that's going to have the most impact. Eventually you will want to practice on both sides.

As your foot hits the obstacle push into it in an upward motion. The aim is to get your center of gravity to go up. Do not apply too much downward pressure as it will cause you to slip. Run into the obstacle and "bounce" up off it.

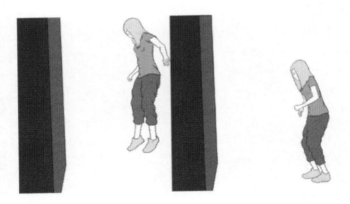

Once you are comfortable add some speed so you can get more height. Don't go too fast too soon otherwise you might just slam into the obstacle.

Jump and plant your foot as high as you can then quickly kick off. If you are too slow to kick off, you will lose power.

If the obstacle is small you can try grabbing onto the edge. If not just touch it as high as you can, keeping in mind that the higher you go the longer the drop back down.

After some practice you will be able to recognize how to react according to the obstacle such as approach speed, when to jump, how high to plant your foot, etc.

Throwing your arms up will give you more reach, as will leading with one arm.

Leaving your hand on the obstacle can be useful to give you a little extra push up as well as to prevent yourself from slamming into it.

WALL POP-UP

The wall pop-up is used to quickly get over or on top of obstacles which are too high to vault over but low enough that you do not feel the need to use the wall climb-up.

It can also be used in conjunction with the wall climb, i.e., once you are in the "up" position of the wall climb, use the pop vault to get on top of the wall.

When first learning the wall pop-up do it on an obstacle that is just a little difficult for you to kong vault over.

The first progression for the wall pop-up is to do it with a crane landing.

Do a vertical wall run on a low wall. Instead of hanging off it, use your arms to give you a boost up. Land in a crane landing. A powerful kick off the wall is essential.

Once you can do that try bringing both feet up to the side.

Finally, you can do the full wall pop-up by bringing both your feet up to land on top of the obstacle.

The movement is like a kong vault.

CORNER WALL RUN

The corner wall run is when you use two walls in a corner to gain extra height. It is like doing a tic-tac off one wall to gain height on the second wall which you then continue to "run" up.

Before attempting the corner wall run you should be proficient with the vertical wall run as well as the tic-tac.

First get comfortable with doing the tic-tac off one wall and then pushing off the other. You will need to be quick to react with your feet.

Decide which wall you want to hit first. If it is on your left side you will use your left foot to come into it, and if it's on your right side you will use your right foot to come into it.

Come in at about a 45° angle and place your foot at about hip level to tic-tac from the first wall into the second.

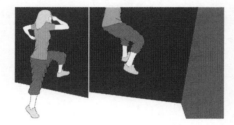

Use your other foot to push back on the second wall (again at about hip level) and then come down to land using a safety tap.

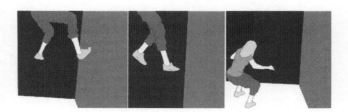

Your arms/hands can help you push on the wall or you can throw them up for more vertical momentum.

Test with the angle you come in on the first wall so you can get the best push off it.

Continue to practice this gradually adding more speed so you can get more height. Also apply basic wall run techniques for more vertical lift.

When you're ready add in the wall run on the second wall so you can reach the top of the obstacle.

Foot placement and explosiveness is the key. You need lots of power and the right angle into the first tic-tac so you can get more momentum off the second step to continue the wall run.

The above pictures show moving from the left wall to the right and then back to the left to grab the top of the obstacle.

An alternative would be to tic-tac off the right wall then do a standard vertical wall run up the left wall to grab the top.

BAR TECHNIQUES

This section covers techniques which are predominantly associated with the bar and have not been covered in previous sections.

STRAIGHT UNDERBAR

The straight underbar allows you to smoothly pass under and/or between bars or other obstacles, e.g., under a ledge.

When first learning the straight underbar you want to progress very slowly. If you go too fast too soon you will probably end up getting injured.

Find an obstacle with a good-sized gap to pass though. Going from low to high will be easier than going from high to low as it will give you more control with your feet on the other side.

When doing the underbar your feet lead the body and your hands grab the obstacle to help control your body as you go through.

Stand next to the bar and stick one leg through, and then the other.

Slowly work your body through. Use this slow speed to become familiar with the distance between your body parts and the obstacle as you go through.

Give extra attention to your back and head as they are most likely to hit. Be very careful you do not hit your head.

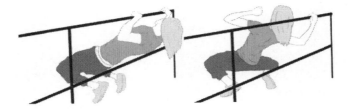

Once you are comfortable gradually get faster and faster. Also try to get straighter with your body, as opposed to side on.

Lead with your feet, lean back a little, and reach forward to grab the bar with your hands so you can pull yourself through.

Lay back as you pull so your upper torso and head can pass through. Direct your legs upwards.

You can swing your legs slightly to the side if needed to avoid hitting your knees or shins.

Next try different variations. Practice high to low, low to high, smaller gaps, more speed, coming from the side, gap jump to underbar, etc.

When you're doing gap jumps to underbars aim with your feet similar to the way you would with a precision jump. Aim them through the gap so the rest of your body will follow along the same path.

Don't lean back too much and as soon as you grab the bar control the rest of your body through.

Note: When you are going under (not between) something about chest to head height doing the underbar is usually unnecessary, but you should still use your hand on the obstacle above you as a guide so that you don't hit your head.

LACHE

The lache is used to swing off a bar (or branch, or anything else you can swing from) and then land in precision, crane, cat, or grab onto another bar (lache to lache).

Knowing how to lache properly will allow you to propel yourself a much greater distance from the bar.

The Swing

The most important part of every lache is swinging. Don't just try to swing with your legs. You need to use your shoulders, chest, torso, etc.

Start in a stationary hang on the bar. Get your feet behind you and curve your spine backwards.

Bend your knees to your chest and then push your feet out and up. Keep your arms straight. This is a flowing movement done in an explosive manner.

Lache to Precision

Once you have the correct swing technique you can attempt the lache to precision. If you don't know how to precision jump yet learn that first.

Like with any precision jump you need to know where you want to land. Choose any spot (line, crack, etc.) on the ground that you are confident to reach.

You also need to be able to see that landing spot as you release your hands. To do this you need to release your hands one at a time.

As your body goes forward release one of your hands and keep it in front of your eyes. When you gain enough speed release your second hand and keep your eyes on the line that you're going to land on.

This arm releasing technique stays the same no matter how far you want to go or what type of lache you are doing. Always release one hand first, then the other.

To precision further you just need to get more momentum in the swing.

Lache to Lache

For the lache to lache instead of focusing on a landing point you need to focus on the next bar you will grab onto.

To do continuous lache to lache you need to grab the next bar with your legs behind you so you maintain enough speed for the next swing.

Start to swing and release your first hand as your legs go in front of you.

As you release your second hand swing your legs behind you.

Then catch the bar.

Your legs swing forward again and then you repeat the movement, lache to lache to lache.

Lache to Cat Leap

The lache to cat leap is a combination of the lache to precision and the lache to lache. It is lache to precision because you have to land on the wall with your legs and it is lache to lache because you will have to grab something with your arms.

If you do not know how to cat leap to cat hang yet learn that first.

The arm release is the same. One hand first then the other. Keep your legs in front of you the whole time so you can absorb the impact as you land in cat.

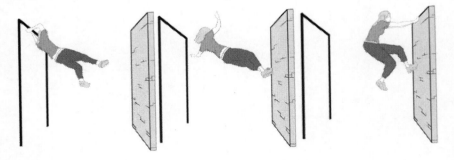

MONKEY TRAVERSE

The monkey traverse (a.k.a. the sloth shimmy) is used to get across long distance obstacles that you can hang off. It is safer than cat-walking on the bar and also works on rope.

Hang below the obstacle suspended by your hands and with both feet crossed over the rope. Your right hand is in front of your left hand and your left foot is in front of your right foot.

Keep a slight bend in your arms and engage your core for the whole time you're are traversing.

Start to move your left hand in front of your right hand.

As your left hand takes grip move your right foot in front of your left. Do not slide your feet. Lift them. This will prevent friction burns.

Ensure your feet land ahead of each other and not on top, otherwise you will get "tangled up".

Continue this motion.

MUSCLE-UPS

Muscle-ups are used to get on top of higher obstacles where a wall climb-up cannot be used, e.g., an overhanging ledge.

You will need to be proficient at the wall climb-up before attempting the muscle up for both technique and conditioning.

The muscle up is quite a physically demanding exercise. Progressing gradually is the key to success.

Start with the hanging knee to elbow leg raise.

Hang off the bar and pull yourself up slightly to retract your shoulder blades. This helps keep you stable while doing the exercise.

Keep your core tight and swing forward a little bit. As your body starts to swing back thrust your knees to your chest.

Next you need to learn how to use the momentum from the hanging knee to elbow raise to pull yourself over the bar.

Start the hanging knee to elbow leg raise as normal. At the height of your back swing pull yourself forward and thrust your knees to your chest whilst allowing your wrists to rotate over the bar.

Allowing your wrists to rotate over the bar is very important.

It will help if you have access to a lower bar to practice the movement. If not, then just keep it in mind when doing the muscle up.

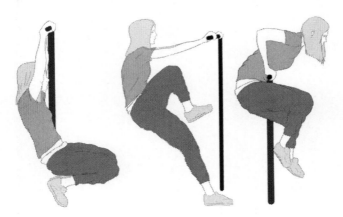

Now you can put everything together to do the muscle up. It is important to utilize everything learnt so far. Remember to keep your core tight.

In addition to retracting your shoulder blades pull your arms forward a little bit when pulling yourself over the bar.

You can use some chalk to get extra grip, although you probably won't have this luxury in "real life" scenarios.

Get some momentum and then thrust your knees to your chest.

As you do so ensure your wrists are loosened and then at the right moment pull yourself up over the bar. Push yourself up until your arms are fully extended.

If this was an obstacle you would bring your foot up and stand just like in the wall-climb.

If you want to do multiple muscle-ups you can use the momentum you gain when lowering yourself down to go into the next repetition.

Once you have built more strength try to do the muscle up with less and less swing until your can do it from a dead hang.

You will also need to practice doing muscle-ups over hanging ledges, i.e., where there is no wall for your feet to push against. To do this you need to adjust your technique a little since you don't have a bar for your wrist to rotate over. Use the "pop" hand movement you use when doing a wall climb-up.

BASIC ROCK CLIMBING

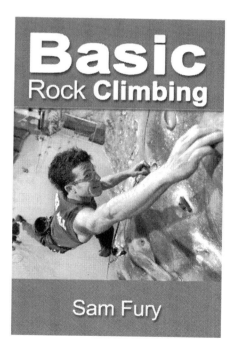

INTRODUCTION

Bouldering the act of climbing without the use of ropes and harnesses.

I have not met many people who did not enjoy climbing when they were a child. Trees, rocks, the family roof, I loved to climb them all, and perhaps you did too. The point is that as children we needed no instruction on how to climb, we just did. That is because climbing is a natural instinct in all of us.

As we get older and stop "practicing" we lose the skills. Luckily, they can be re-learnt, and in the process we can also learn the best methods to use.

The only intention for the climbing techniques described in this section is to give an introduction to the basic maneuvers and foundational techniques needed for bouldering.

Actually, the basics are all you really need. Learn the basics and practice.

Safety Note: When bouldering, NEVER climb higher than you would be willing to jump down. It is also wise to use a crash mat.

It is a good idea to learn the safety tap (see it in the Safety chapter of Essential Parkour Training).

BASIC PRINCIPLES

Holds are what you place your feet and hands onto when climbing. They are what you "hold" on to.

Climb With Your Legs

Your legs are your main climbing tool. Your arms are primarily for keeping balance.

Move your feet up the wall first and use your legs to push you up.

Know where you will place your foot before moving it.

Place your foot carefully and firmly.

Use the edges of your feet or the ball of your big toe.

Press your foot firmly downwards and into the wall.

Trust that you can stand.

Plan Your Route

Plan your route before you start climbing and at least one move ahead whilst climbing. Adjust your plan as needed as you are climbing.

Climb Smooth

Climb smooth and fluid. Don't pause between moves.

Step lightly and only reach as much as needed to grab the hold.

Grip only as hard as you need to.

Breathe.

Gaining Reach

Reach Backwards

Turn away from the hold and reach backwards for it. It is similar to reaching for something far under a bed.

Stand Up

Stand straight and keep your hips close to the wall with you weight over your feet, as opposed to leaning against the rock.

Bumping

Gain momentum off one hold in order to reach a better one.

HOLDS AND GRIPS

Edges

A horizontal hold with an edge you can grab onto.

Often flat but sometimes has a lip which you can pull on.

Crimp Grip

Crimping is grabbing the edge with your fingertips flat and your fingers arched above the tips.

Crimping too hard can cause tendon damage.

Full Crimp

To do the full crimp, place the pads of your fingertips on an edge and curl your fingers so that the second joint is sharply flexed.

Press your thumb on top of the index finger's fingernail to secure the grip.

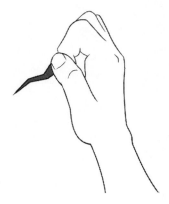

Half Crimp

If you let your thumb press against the side of your index finger, you are using the half crimp.

The half crimp is weaker but less damaging to your fingers. If you have the option, use the half crimp.

Slopers

Slopers are rounded handholds without an edge.

They are easiest to grab if they are above you.

Keep your arms straight for maximum leverage when gripping them.

Open Hand Grip

To grab a sloper use the open hand grip.

Use the friction of your skin against the rock surface.

Feel around with your fingers to find grip spots.

Wrap your hand onto the hold with your fingers close together.

Feel around with your thumb to see if there is a bump that you can press against.

Pinches

Pinches are holds which can be gripped by pinching with your fingers on one side and your thumb opposed on the other.

If the pinch hold is small, use your thumb opposed to your index finger with your middle finger stacked on top.

With larger pinch holds, oppose your thumb with all your fingers.

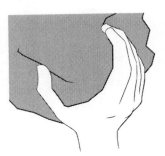

Side Pulls

Side pulls are holds that you pull sideways instead of straight down, due to their orientation.

You can pull outward on the side pull while pushing a foot in the opposite direction to keep you in place.

Pockets

Pockets are holes in the rock surface which you can place your finger(s) in.

Insert as many fingers as you can comfortably fit into a pocket. Use your strongest fingers first.

Feel inside the pocket to find a surface you can pull against.

Gastons

A hold oriented either vertically or diagonally and is usually to your front.

Grab it with your fingers and palm facing into the rock and your thumb pointing downward.

Bend your elbow at a sharp angle and point it away from your body.

Crimp your fingers on the edge and pull outward.

Undercling

Any hold that is gripped on its underside. It requires body tension and opposition.

Grip the rock with your palm facing up and your thumb pointing out.

Pull out on the undercling and push your feet against the wall.

Palming

If no handhold exists keep your hand in place by pushing into a dimple in the rock with the heel of your palm.

Matching Hands

Matching hands is when you place your hands next to each other on the same hold so you can change hands.

A similar technique can be done with your feet. Do so by slowly replacing one foot with the other and without jumping.

It can also be done with a hand and foot.

Plan ahead to minimize matching, e.g., reach for an extra hold over so that your trailing hand can have its own hold.

FOOT TECHNIQUES

Smearing

Push the flat of your foot hard on the wall, using friction to hold you up.

If you want to go up direct the force slightly downwards.

Return to a foothold as soon as you can.

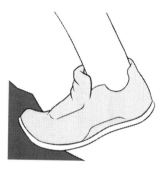

Back Stepping

Step on a hold so that the outside of your hip faces into the rock, allowing for longer reach in the same direction as the foot that you stepped back with.

Drop one knee toward the ground with the other pointing up for an exaggerated back step.

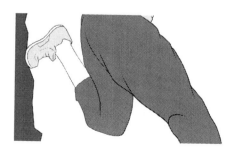

Flagging

Flagging is used to balance your body when reaching for a hold.

Cross one foot behind the other to avoid swinging out from the rock.

Mantle

Use the mantle to climb up onto a ledge.

Get up close to the ledge.

Pull yourself up, rock sideways, turn your hand around and push yourself up until you can place a foot and stand up.

Exercises such as pulls-ups and muscle-ups will help build the strength needed to do mantles. These are detailed in the Parkour section of this manual.

Stemming

Stemming is used to climb opposing walls, otherwise known as chimneys.

Press a foot into one of the walls and your other foot against the other.

Push out with opposing force to hold your weight up.

Do the same with your hands.

Hold your weight with your arms/hands and shift both feet up.

Once you have a good grip with your feet, hold your weight with your legs and move your hands up.

Repeat this 'shuffling' with your hands and feet to climb the chimney.

Hooking

Heel and toe hooks can aid in balance and provide leverage for movement.

There are a few ways to use the hook, e.g.:

With your foot to climb onto a ledge.

Hooking under a rock to keep stability whilst negotiating an overhang.

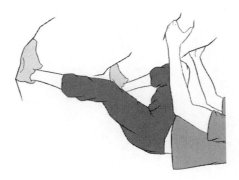

TYPES OF FACES

Slabs

A slab is any rock face than is angled at less than 90°.

Keep your weight centered on your feet.

Stand upright on the rock and away from the slab surface.

Make small steps on small footholds rather than big steps on big holds.

Plan three to five of your intended foot holds ahead at a time.

Aim for big holds and rest when you reach them.

As you climb look for variations in the surface and smear on tiny holds.

Be precise with your toe placement.

Feel the hold with a finger to find the best spot for your foot placement.

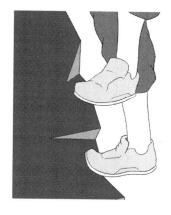

Vertical

Vertical faces are angled at 90°, i.e., straight up, (or close to it).

Keep your weight over your feet as much as possible.

Use an upright body position.

Use your hands and arms for pulling if needed.

Overhangs

Overhangs are rock faces that are overhung or angled more than 90°.

Heel and toe hooks are useful to take the weight off your arms.

CRACK CLIMBING

Climb the natural cracks in the rock by jamming. Jamming is wedging your body parts into a crack.

Doing so can cut your hands. Prevent this by taping your hands for protection.

Hand Jam

Wedge the side of your hand in the crack with your thumb on top.

Tuck your thumb into the palm of your hand.

Expand your hand to exert opposing pressure against the walls of the crack.

Hang your weight off your wedged hand.

Foot Jam

Once your hands are jammed into the crack lift a foot and push the front part of your shoe into the crack.

Stand up on the jammed foot.

Step the other foot up to calf level and jam it in the crack.

Shuffling

Move upward by shuffling your hands up the crack. There are three ways to do this.

- Move your top hand up first, then the lower one below it.
- Lift the bottom hand out of the crack and hand jam above your upper hand.
- Use the above two techniques together.

Do the same with your feet.

SURVIVAL SWIMMING

INTRODUCTION

Swimming is a very important skill when it comes to survival. There are too many stories of people that have drowned needlessly because they didn't know how to swim efficiently in specific situations.

Swimming is also fun and beneficial to the body. It is a low impact form of exercise with great cardiovascular advantages.

This book was first published in 2014. It was an instructional manual on how to learn the best swimming strokes for survival. It is updated in 2018 by combining the original contents with part 1 and sections of part 2 of the Swim Workouts and Water Rescue manual.

This book is split into 3 parts.

Efficient Swimming

This section has techniques and training methods for improving your ability in swimming:

- Fast
- Long distance
- Underwater (speed and distance)

Swimming in Open Water

Being near any body of water has its inherent dangers, and open water has even more. This section has information on the different dangers in various forms of open water and the best ways to swim in them.

In this manual, the term "open water" refers to any natural body of water such as oceans, lakes, and rivers.

Learn to Swim

This is the original Survival Swimming book. It is for people learning how to swim and teaches basic skills and strokes.

Logically, this should be part 1. I made it part 3 because I do not encourage people trying to learn to swim from a book. If you really cannot swim, take some swimming classes from a professional teacher in a controlled environment.

I did consider not putting this section in the manual at all, but decided to for those that don't have access to swim classes. The dry land exercises can be safely done by anyone. And, under the supervision of a responsible and capable swimmer, you could do the water-based exercises also.

GENERAL WATER SAFETY

The activities in this manual can be dangerous if you do not take the proper precautions. Follow the water safety guidelines in this and other sections.

Important! Whenever possible, learn new techniques in calm waters (such as a pool). Only when you are confident should you practice them in open water.

- The best way to ensure safety is to avoid the danger in the first place. If total avoidance is not an option, the next best thing is to seek out local knowledge. Ask lifeguards, local surfers, paddlers, fisherman, etc. Also, scout it out yourself as circumstances may change.
- Always have a safety person present, e.g., a training partner or lifeguard.
- Protect yourself from the sun with appropriate clothing and sunscreen.
- Stay hydrated.
- Keep warm. This is covered in detail in Part 2 of this manual.
- Don't go near water under the influence of drugs or alcohol.
- It is good to push yourself for improvement, but be careful not to push yourself too much. This is especially true in open water.
- Have the correct safety and rescue equipment nearby, and know how to use it.
- Train only in waters and conditions you know to be safe. Look for signs and flags for the information you need, and if you are unsure, ask the lifeguards. Don't swim when the red flag is flying.
- Watch out for other people doing recreational activities, such as surfing or motorsports. Usually, they will have separate designated areas from swimmers.

- Never run or dive into the unknown water. In open water, you must always check as conditions can change.
- If you get into trouble, stay calm and raise your arm to signal for help.
- Always wear a life vest when in a boat or any uncontrolled environment. Zip it up! A loose vest can get caught on many things.
- Tell someone that is not going with you where you will be training and when you expect to be back.
- Take care near any water edge whether it be a pool, riverbank, etc.
- Learn about the different characteristics of various water bodies before training in them.
- Enter and exit the water in a safe manner using the designated entry and exit points, e.g., the ladder. Use your hands and feet, and take your time.

EFFICIENT SWIMMING

This section has techniques and training methods for improving your ability in swimming:

- Fast
- Long distance
- Underwater (speed and distance)

TREADING WATER

Treading water is the most energy-efficient way to stay in one spot.

Learn to tread water before doing any other water-based training. This is so if you need to you can tread water until you either create a plan for self-rescue or help arrives.

When first learning to tread water, do so in shallow water and with a lifeguard present. Progress to deep water when confident.

While treading water your body is vertical in the water and your head is above the surface. Your arms and legs work to keep you afloat. Torso movement is minimal.

There are a few ways to tread water. The following method is a little harder to get the hang of but it is the most energy efficient. It combines vertical sculling with your arms and the eggbeater kick.

Sculling

To skull, move your arms horizontal in the water, back and forth — not up and down.

Turn your palms in the direction that your arms are moving. Angle your thumbs a little up on the way in, and your pinky fingers a little up on the way out.

Keep your back straight. Don't lean forward or backward.

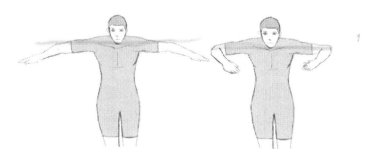

Vary the width of your stroke. Sometimes your hands remain far apart, and sometimes they almost come together.

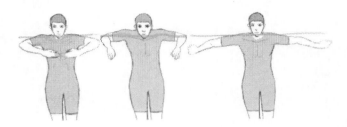

You can start by practicing this in shallow water. Find a depth where you can keep your head above water whilst you kneel down.

Begin the sculling action with your hands, enough to raise your knees off the bottom.

When you are ready, move into deeper water. Have your feet directly underneath you, toes pointing straight down.

Eggbeater Kick (Rotary Kick)

The egg-beater kick can be tricky to learn but it is worth going through the trouble. In comparison to the alternatives (such as the flutter kick), it is the most energy efficient.

Move your legs like an eggbeater, each leg rotating a different direction. It is like a breast-stroke kick done one leg at a time. When one leg kicks out, the other should be coming in.

To begin learning the egg-beater kick do it on dry land by sitting on the edge of a chair. Sit up straight and move only your right leg in a counter-clockwise circle.

Next, move only your left leg in a clockwise circle.

When you are ready, join these two leg movements together. As your right leg goes out, your left leg comes in. At all times one leg comes in while the other goes out.

Once you have the coordination, practice the egg-beater kick in the water.

Lift your toes as you press down, so that your flat foot pushes down on the water, helping to propel you up.

Also, point your toes as you bring your foot up so that you have less resistance.

Do not extend your legs completely. If they become straight you will lose upwards propulsion.

Treading Water

Once proficient at sculling and the eggbeater kick you can stay afloat by doing ONLY one or the other.

You can perform tasks with your hands while staying afloat in one spot, and/or you can stay afloat in case of a leg injury.

By putting the two actions together you conserve energy in both your arms and legs. This is ideal in a survival situation when you need to stay in one spot for long periods of time.

When treading water, stay calm and slow down your breathing rhythm. This will maximize your conservation of energy.

SWIMMING FAST

You will need to swim fast in emergency situations such as rescue or escape. Race swimming techniques are a base. They are then adapted for use in emergency situations.

There are three basic elements to consider when your goal is swimming fast.

1. Entry and/or Initial propulsion
2. Underwater swim
3. Surface swimming

Your initial propulsion is usually either a dive entry or by pushing off something.

Once you have your initial propulsion you want to swim as fast and for as long as you can underwater. Use the fly-kick (either dolphin or fish tale).

Swimming underwater is faster than surface swimming due to less resistance. When speed is your goal, swim underwater for as long as possible.

Finally, once you need to surface for air, use freestyle (a.k.a. over-arm, front-crawl) since it is the fastest surface-swimming stroke.

It is assumed that you already know the basics of the above three elements. Now we concentrate on improvement in the two factors needed to maximize speed for each element, i.e.,

- Decreasing drag
- Improving propulsion

Entry and Initial Propulsion

There are different entry and/or initial propulsion techniques which you can use. The one you choose depends on the situation.

- Push-off
- Shallow dive
- Dolphin dive
- Deep-water floating start
- Flip Turn and push-off

When speed is your primary goal, all these actions will lead into the underwater fly-kick.

Note: When you need to enter unknown waters, use the safe entry techniques described in Part 2 of this manual. Opting for a safer entry technique may slow you down, but you won't be very fast at swimming if you get injured. Safety first, always.

Push-off / Streamlined Position

For the greatest speed when pushing-off the edge, drop below the water 1 to 3 feet. When doing a flip turn this will be automatic.

The best position for your legs/feet is shoulder width apart and with a bend in your knees. Push hard off the edge with strong legs and a tight core.

When you push off your body must be as streamlined as possible. Become a straight arrow, stretching your body from your toes to your fingertips.

Place the palm of one hand on the back of the other. Wrap your upper hand's pinky and thumb around your lower hand and then raise them over your head. Point your fingers in the direction you are going.

Straighten your arms. Tuck them behind your head and squeeze your shoulder blades together. Another method is to squeeze your ears between your biceps.

Keep your head down (swimming down-hill) with the top of your head pointing in the direction you want to go.

Point your feet and turn your toes in towards each other a little (pigeon-toed).

Keep your chin tucked and use a smooth exhale in whatever way is most comfortable for you.

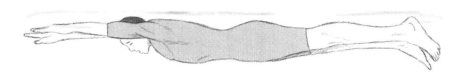

Maintain this streamline position as you push off the wall. Start the underwater fly-kick to maintain momentum underwater before surfacing into freestyle.

Note: Being on your side (as opposed to facing down) creates less resistance and you may gain some speed. You should experiment with this.

Diving

Diving will give you the most propulsion but is also the most dangerous entry method.

Important! If you are unsure of the water depth and/or what lies below the surface, DO NOT DIVE!

In an emergency situation, you may be pretty sure it is safe to dive but do not have the time for a thorough assessment. For this reason, use the shallow dive.

A shallow dive is when you "arc" into the water hands first whilst you adopt the streamlined position.

When starting to perfect your dive, do so from a stationary position. Place your lead (strongest) leg on the edge of the water (e.g. poolside) with your toes a little over the edge. Your rear foot is flat on the ground.

Balance your weight evenly on both feet. Place your arms above your head in the streamlined position, with your chin tucked to your chest.

Push off with your lead foot so you get some distance. Arc over as you push.

Adopt the streamline position as you enter the water.

Once you are in the water, hold your head up and arch your back. This will steer your body up away from the bottom.

The more you arch, the more speed you will lose. You have to compromise depending on the water depth. Also remember, that you will be faster streamlining a couple of feet below the surface.

Note: Do not look/arch up before you are in the water. You will lose speed and may get injured.

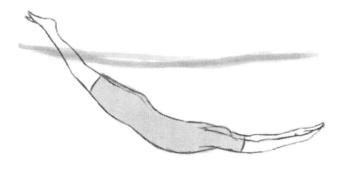

When you're ready, try diving from a walking and then a running start. In this case, your arms will start by your sides. Once you leap off the edge adopt the correct position so you can enter the water using the same basic form.

Dolphin Dive

Dolphin dives are useful when running into the water in a beach scenario. It will allow you to overcome waist/chest deep water as fast as possible. Run until the water is knee/waist high and then use the dolphin dive.

As you run in, be vigilant for obstacles in the terrain, e.g., rocks or holes. Once you hit the water, lift your feet completely out of the water for as long as possible. This decreases "drag time".

Put your hands in the streamline position and leap/arc over into a dive. Do this before the water decreases your forward momentum. Roughly knee to waist deep.

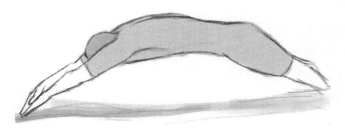

Don't dive too hard (you might injure yourself) but dive deep enough to grab the sand on the bottom. Grab hold of the sand and lock your feet in one in front of the other. Push forward off the ground as fast as you can into your next dolphin dive. Continue to dolphin dive in rapid succession until it is too deep to continue (about neck deep).

Do not look up whilst dolphin diving. Like in the shallow dive, this is important for safety and speed.

If a wave is approaching, dolphin dive under it, grab the sand and stay under until the wave passes over you.

Once it is too deep to dolphin dive, transition into the underwater fly-kick.

You can use the dolphin dive to come back into shore also. Swim until it is shallow enough to dolphin dive, then continue to dolphin dive until you can run out.

Floating Start

Use a floating start from a floating/treading position when you have nothing to push off.

The key for this is to use an explosive initial kick (such as a side scissor kick) and then go straight into freestyle.

If you know that you will need a floating start, get as close to the freestyle position as possible.

Adopt a horizontal position. Place your dominant hand in front, ready to pull back into your first stroke. Have your other arm in a half-stroke position. Your heels should be close to the surface of the water. Tread water in this position.

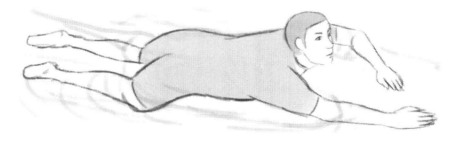

When it is time to swim kick hard as you pull with your first stroke and transition into normal freestyle.

Flip Turns

Flip turns are often identified with swimming races in a pool. In an emergency situation having to turn in the water is not likely, but it is possible. Knowing how to flip turn will make it much faster.

First, learn the flip turn without having to push off the wall. In an emergency situation, this is most likely the style you will use, and it also makes it easier to learn.

The main flip part of the flip turn is actually only a half-flip. Start by swimming on your stomach (e.g., freestyle). As your arm enters the water for the turn, start a half-flip by tucking your chin and doing a small dolphin kick. At the same time, move your hands to your sides. Breath out through your nose to prevent any water getting up it.

Continue the half-flip by tucking your knees towards your eyes and your feet to your bum. At the same time, push down with the palms of your hands to get your feet over your head. Keep your elbows close to your body while doing this.

As you complete the half-flip, bring your arms into the streamline position. You are now pointing in your new direction of travel.

Roll onto your stomach by twisting your hands a little and looking in the direction you want to rotate. Don't turn your head, only move your eyes.

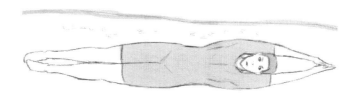

Use an explosive kick and arm pull to set you off in your new direction like you would in a floating start.

Note: Don't try to look where you are going during the flip. It will slow you down and mess up your co-ordination. Look at your knees instead.

To turn and push off a wall (such as in a pool swimming race) speed up (kick harder) when you are about 5 meters away from the wall. Ensure you have enough air to make the turn, but don't take a breath before it as you will slow down.

Once you are a bit more than an arm's length away from the wall, do the turn as normal. Push off the wall as described before (Push-off / Streamlined Position). The difference is that you will be face up when you do the push off, toes pointing up.

Once you push off, start to turn onto your stomach and then do underwater fly-kicks.

You may wish to start to fly-kick before (whilst on your back) and/or during your turn also. Experiment to discover what you prefer/works best for you.

Continue to fly-kick until you need to start surface swimming.

Once you can do the basic turn and push off, work on perfecting your distance in relation to the wall. Land your feet with your knees bent close to 90° and your hips bent close to 110°.

Underwater Fly Kick

When you know how to do it, swimming underwater is faster than swimming on the surface of it. When you want to go fast, swim underwater for as long as you can.

The fastest way to swim underwater is using the underwater fly-kick.

There are two main ways to do the underwater fly-kick. The dolphin kick and the fish kick.

If you are good at it, the fish kick is faster than the dolphin kick, but in the SFP we focus on the dolphin kick because it is:

- Easier to master.
- Easier to control, especially in open water.
- Used in other strokes outlined in this manual.

Once you have the standard dolphin kick mastered, you may wish to progress to the fish-tale kick.

After your initial propulsion (e.g., dive or push-off) maintain your streamline position. You want to maximize this glide phase before you start kicking.

Just before you start to slow down, use both feet/legs at the same time to kick up and down. Keep your upper body in the streamline position.

Bend your knees so that your kicks finish/start well in front (or behind) your body, but do not kick from your knees. Use your core/hips to generate the power. To do this, suck in your tummy and squeeze your buttocks together.

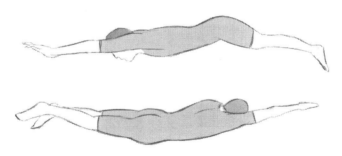

You must also snap your toes and ankle. It may help to think of your body as a whip. The power comes from your core (the handle), and your feet/toes are the tip of the whip which snap up and down. Kick fast and kick small.

Ensure you also kick backward instead of only up and down. You want to push the water behind you.

Your up and down kicks should be of equal force. Use the vertical kicking drill to develop your coordination and strength for this. The vertical kicking drill is in the freestyle chapter.

When you start to surface, begin freestyle.

Ankle Strength and Flexibility

Increasing your ankle strength and flexibility will improve your dolphin (and flutter) kick. Here are some exercises you can do.

Ankle rotations. Move your foot and ankle in a circle as large as possible without pain. Do 15-20 circles in each direction.

Ankle stretches. There are four levels of this exercise. Each increases in difficulty from the previous one.

From a standing position, place the top of your toes on the ground a half step behind your other foot. Push down and forward into the ground.

Sit on your heels, with your shins and the top of your feet flat on the ground.

Lean back onto your hands to increase the stretch.

Finally, put your hands up in the streamline position and then lift your knees off the ground.

Ankle Inversion. From a standing position, roll one foot to the outside. Press the edge of your foot into the ground in a gentle manner. Only do one foot at a time.

Freestyle

This chapter assumes you already know the basic mechanics of swimming freestyle. If you don't, please see part 3 of this manual.

Freestyle (overarm) is the fastest way to surface swim. By improving your technique, you will become faster and more energy efficient.

There are a few different areas which you can "tweak". Practice in each individual area, and then put them all together when you are ready.

Balance

Being balanced in the water will make you more streamlined and so will increase your speed.

Maintain a position that is as horizontal as possible.

Except when taking a breath, keep your head down and your neck relaxed. Imagine you have a blowhole in the back of your neck that you have to keep open. Looking down (as opposed to forwards) will also help.

Breathing

Breathing while swimming (as opposed to holding your breath under-water) increases your stamina. Start blowing out as soon as you finish inhaling and continue to do so until you take your next breath.

Experiment with breathing rhythms (e.g. take a breath every 3rd or 5th stroke) to see what works best for you. It may help to count your arm strokes (e.g., 1, 2, 3, 4, breathe) or whatever method you prefer.

It is important to completely exhale before taking your next breath so that you get rid of all the stale air. This increases your stamina and keeps you streamlined for longer. Every time you breathe you are breaking your streamlined position.

Keep as close as possible to your streamlined position while breathing. Do this by turning your head as opposed to lifting it out of the water. Your mouth only needs to be a little bit out of the water to inhale. Your eye line should be no higher than to the side. If you're looking to the sky, you are turning your head way too much.

Breathing on alternate sides of your body (bilaterally) is a good habit.

Always inhale through your mouth, but try to exhale most of the air through your nose.

This is especially true when turning/flipping to avoid getting water up your nose.

Rolling

Roll from side to side with each arm stroke. This will engage your back muscles and improve propulsion.

Engage your core as you do it.

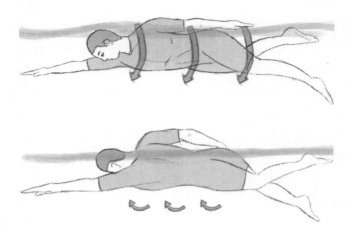

Rolling Drills

This drill is good for getting used to floating on your sides.

Float flat on your back and do a light flutter kick for propulsion. Keep your body straight with your arms at your sides. Apply downward pressure on the back of your head and on your shoulder blades so that your hips and legs buoy up.

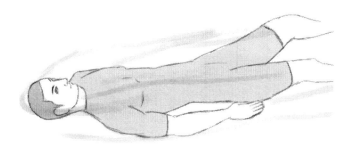

Once you feel balanced in this position, do the following:

- Roll onto your side so that your top arm and some of your top thigh clear the water.
- Your head does not move while you roll on your side. Keep looking at the sky and roll your body as one.
- Continue to flutter kick.

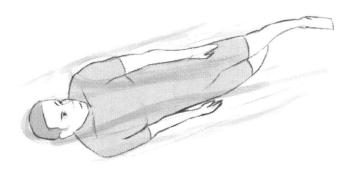

Roll as far as you are comfortable. A 45° body roll is good for most people.

Practice this on both sides of your body.

Once you are comfortable with the above, advance by rolling to 90° so you face down.

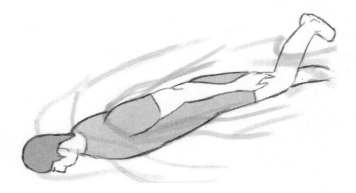

Keep flutter kicking and keep balanced. Continue to roll in the same direction until you are in the 45° body position, but on your opposite side.

Remember to roll your whole body together. Don't lead with your head.

When balanced, roll back the other way.

Arm Technique

The freestyle stroke is explained in four parts. The catch, pull, exit, and recovery. These four stages occur and repeat in the order listed.

There is a more advanced arm stroke known as the Early Vertical Forearm Position (EVF). It is harder to master, holds a greater risk of injury, and the gain in speed is minimal. It is more for elite competitive swimmers.

The following technique is like a non-extreme EVF.

Catch

The catch is when your hand first enters the water.

Create a "web" with your hand by spacing your fingers apart a little, about 30% of the diameter of one finger. Keep this spacing for the whole time.

As you roll your body, lengthen your arm out with your palm faced down. Angle your fingertips a little downward and flex your wrist. Point your middle finger in your direction of travel.

Enter your hand into the water fingertips first. Ensure your arm/hand does not cross your centerline.

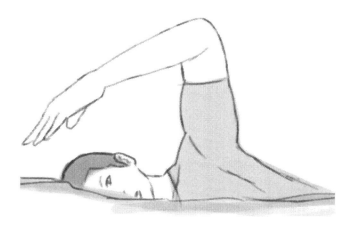

Once your hand is in the water, bend your elbow and press back on the water. Your forearm is in a near-vertical position.

Do not push forward once your hand is in the water. It is better to go straight into the pull phase of the stroke.

It may help to imagine your arm is moving over a big ball.

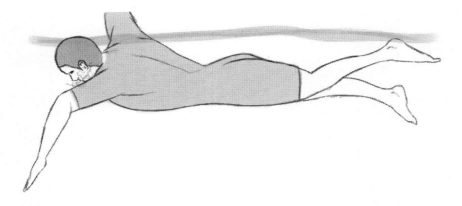

You can use finger paddles to help you perfect your catch. Wear them loose.

If you over-reach or have some other bad technique, the finger paddle will come off.

Another thing you can do is use a kick-board. Focus on a good catch with only one arm. The kick-board will prevent you reaching forward.

Pull

The pull is the movement of your arm in the water down the length of your body.

After doing a good catch your elbow will be in the "high" position. Your elbow faces the sky and your palm faces to your rear.

Keep this high elbow as you push the water behind you.

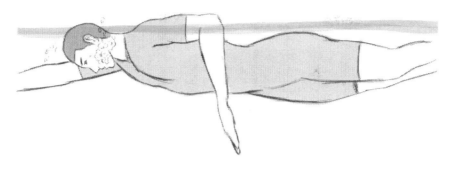

A good catch and pull is an easy, flowing feeling. You get great forward propulsion utilizing your pecks and lats.

Exit

This phase of your stroke is when your arm/hand leaves the water, just past your hip.

It is important not to be too eager to bring your arm out of the water. Push beyond your hip as if you are trying to reach your knee, using the same press-up motion you would when exiting a pool on the wall.

Do this push for the whole range of your pull, and as your thumb touches your thigh, flick the water out.

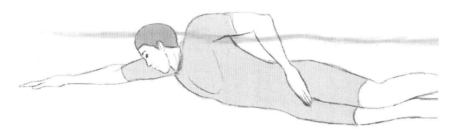

Recovery

The recovery is the time when your arm is in the air. It flicks out of the exit and then re-enters into the catch.

It is best not to think about your recovery. Let it take its natural path. Your mental effort is better spent focusing on a great catch.

You can use stretch cords to practice all phases of your stroke on dry land. It is also useful for focusing on problem areas.

Efficient Kicking

A good kick is a compact one. It shouldn't be too low nor break the water's surface. Do not disturb your natural body alignment.

Move your feet/legs independently of each other. Push one down as you pull the other up. Putting energy into both the up and down strokes is important.

Use short, quick kicks with your whole leg, starting at the hip. Keep your legs long and straight, but not rigid. Have a slight, natural bend in your knees.

Point your toes behind you but keep your ankles relaxed. Only the bottom of your feet meet the water's surface.

Find a rhythm that is comfortable and stick with it. Around 15 kicks every 10 seconds is good.

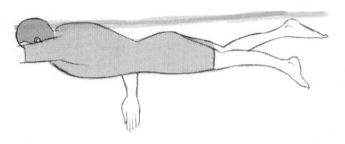

Vertical Kicking Drill

This vertical kicking drill will help to improve your flutter kick. It is also good for your dolphin kick.

Do this drill in deep water, but make sure you are near something you can hold onto when you get tired.

Be vertical in the water and do nothing but flutter kicking to keep your mouth and nose above the surface. You will be kicking hard. Concentrate on correct kicking technique as described before.

Begin with your arms underwater and use a small sculling motion.

As you improve, try keeping your arms and hands tight against your body.

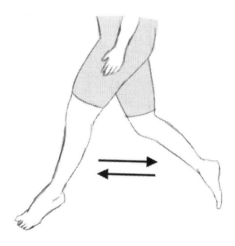

Advance further by raising your fingertips out of the water. Raise your arms higher and higher as you gain strength.

Transitioning from the Fly Kick to Freestyle

As you begin to surface begin to flutter kick and start to pull one of your arms down from the streamline position. Time the completion of your pull phase so that you arm exits the water as if you were doing freestyle all along. This takes practice.

Complete a few strokes before taking a breath and then continue into freestyle as normal.

Additional Tips for Improvement

You can adapt most of these tips to all areas of swimming, and life in general.

- **Train regularly,** at least twice a week.
- **Compete against your times.** Notice what causes you to swim faster and use what works best for you.
- **Identify and work on your weak points.**
- **Visualize someone chasing you.** Feel as if you are being chased, then work on calming your mind and body and concentrate on swimming as fast as you can.
- **Get a professional swim coach.** For those of you that are having difficulties or want to get to the next level.

SWIMMING LONG DISTANCE

There are two strokes to learn for swimming long-distance. Survival backstroke, and the combat side stroke.

Survival backstroke, a.k.a. elementary backstroke is an easy stroke to learn and is very energy efficient. It is for long distance and/or survival situations, e.g., waiting for rescue.

The combat side stroke (CSS) is an ultra-efficient variation of the sidestroke. It was developed by the navy seals and is perfect for escape, evasion, and survival.

- It is efficient (fast yet energy conserving)
- You can do it with gear (like a backpack)
- Your body profile is less (you'll be harder to see)
- It is excellent for swimming through the surf in open water
- You can observe your surroundings as you swim (unlike the survival backstroke)

Survival Backstroke

This chapter assumes you know the basic mechanics of survival backstroke. If you need to learn it from scratch, please see part 3 of this manual.

Survival backstroke is floating on your back as you propel through the water. You use a simultaneous frog/breaststroke kick and a sculling motion with your hands. Your arms and legs move and come together at the same time.

The main goal of the survival backstroke is to conserve energy and reduce heat loss.

To maximize energy conservation, do the survival backstroke very slow. Take short strokes and glide for as long as possible. Only take the next stroke when you feel your legs dropping or you loose forward momentum.

Taking short strokes minimizes heat loss from under your armpits and between your legs. Your arms should not extend beyond your shoulders.

Also, at the end of each stroke, bring your arms and legs together.

Hold them close but comfortable against your body.

Also use the survival backstroke is if an underwater explosion is likely. You will want to go faster so you can escape the blast, so make your strokes larger. Take your next stroke sooner than normal, but not too soon.

Make the most out of your streamlined glide position while achieving the most speed.

Combat Side Stroke

Combat Side Stroke (CSS) is a mix of freestyle, breaststroke, and sidestroke.

There are 4 basic stages to the CSS. The streamline position, two catch and pull movements, and the recovery. The recovery involves a scissor kick paired with a breaststroke-like arm movement.

Note: A lot of the terminology used in this chapter is explained in the freestyle section.

Streamline Position

Get some initial propulsion. Adopt the streamline position as explained in the Entry and Initial Propulsion chapter.

First Catch and Pull

Do your first catch by pressing the palm of your top hand down. If you are rolling to your right, then your right hand is/will be on top. Bend your arm at the elbow.

Ensure to keep your arm aligned at a downward angle. Your shoulder is at the top, your elbow below that, then your wrist, and finally your fingers at the bottom. Doing this will maximize your first pull.

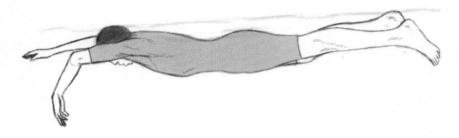

Continue the catch as you rotate onto your side. Your forearm is vertical, elbow above your wrist.

Stay on your side until your recovery stage.

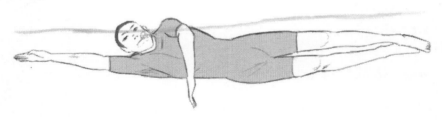

Flow into the pull by continuing the movement of your top arm until your hand is in line with your upper thigh. Your hand follows your midline. Be careful not to raise your elbow too high.

At this stage, your arm is almost fully extended. Do not let your hand come out of the water.

Now is a good time to take a breath. When you exhale, do so in a slow and steady manner.

Second Catch and Pull

Start your second catch and pull with your other arm by sweeping it down. Your palm faces down and stays fixed in that position. As you sweep down it creates resistance against the water, propelling you forward.

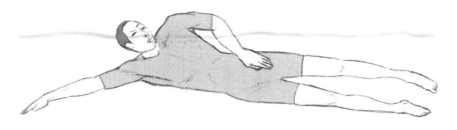

When your arm is vertical, your palm will be facing to your rear.

Continue the arc of your bottom arm until your hand is on your thigh.

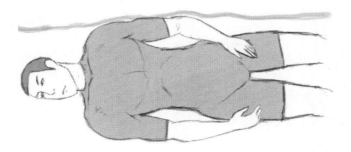

The catch, pull, and recovery of your lower arm is almost identical to a breaststroke motion.

Note: As you do the second pull you can either leave your head up breathing or look back down. If you have a tendency to sink you are better off looking back down.

Recovery

Start the recovery with a simultaneous scissor kick and arm movement.

Bring both your arms up through the center-line of your body. They then travel back into the streamline position, like breaststroke. Keep your arms and hands underwater and as close to your body as possible.

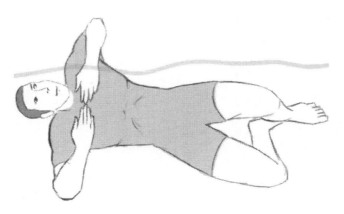

Continue your arms forward past your face as you do the scissor kick. Finish in the streamlined position.

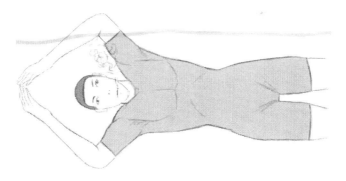

Scissor Kick

Do the scissor kick as you bring your arms forward. This helps with propulsion and corkscrew's your body back into the streamline position.

Move your top leg forward and your bottom leg backward at the same time. Bring them back together in the streamlined position. Keep your toes flexed towards your shin until you adopt the streamlined position.

Draw your top knee up so there is a 90° angle at your hip and knee. At the same time, bend your bottom leg back at the knee.

Extend the lower part of your top leg in front of your torso as you kick your bottom leg back.

Point your toes once you have extended your legs, then draw them into the streamline position.

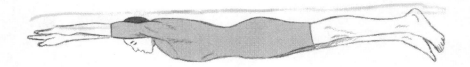

Slowly exhale as you glide in the streamline position. Be sure to get the most out of the glide before starting the next arm cycle.

If speed is more important you can flutter kick before initiating your first pull again. You could also use the sprinter's CSS.

Sprinter's CSS

Use the sprinter's CSS when you need to go faster. The tradeoff is that you will use more energy since will use a greater stroke count over the same distance.

To do the sprinter's CSS do a half stroke on your second pull. Everything else stays the same.

From the start of the second pull, bring your arm down as normal until it is almost at a right angle to your body.

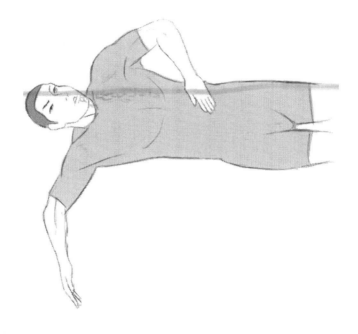

Instead of pulling it all the way to your thigh, scoop it up into your armpit.

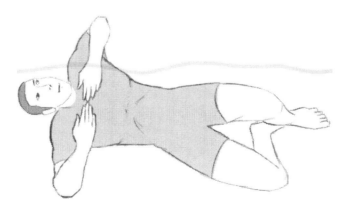

From here, push it forward into a full extension as normal.

Guide Stroke

Use the guide stroke to check your direction when using the CSS to swim a long distance.

It uses a breaststroke-type movement for your arms and the dolphin kick for your legs.

Start in the streamline position.

Push your palms out against the water to a position a little wider than your shoulders.

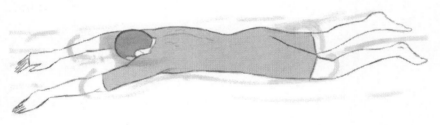

Press your palms against the water as you rotate your hands and lower arms into a vertical position.

Your finger-tips point down and your palms angle toward your chest.

Pull your palms towards your chest.

This creates forward propulsion and allows you to raise your head above the surface. Now you can breathe and look around.

Try not to lift your head too far out of the water.

This will cause your hips and legs to sink, which will decrease your momentum.

Recover your arms back to the streamline position as you would with breast-stroke. Keep them close to your body along your centerline.

As you recover your arms, use the downward motion of the dolphin kick. This helps with propulsion back into the streamline position. From here you can continue into CSS or another guide stroke.

Note: For more instruction on the dolphin kick, see the underwater fly-kick chapter.

If you get disorientated, tread water until you figure out which direction you need to swim in.

SWIMMING LONG DISTANCE UNDERWATER

There are two major factors when it comes to swimming long distance underwater:

1. Efficient stroke.
2. Lung capacity (how long you can hold your breath for).

This section is a 5 stage training plan. Use it to increase your ability to swim long distance underwater. The aim is to swim 50 meters underwater.

Important! Depriving yourself of oxygen is dangerous. Safe training is paramount!

Safety

Here are some safety pointers when practicing to swim long distance underwater.

- Train with a partner, and not at the same time. Your friend must watch you so he can help if something goes wrong. If you must train alone, then at the very least make sure there is a lifeguard present.
- Stay in shallow water, especially to begin with.
- Never push yourself to beat your last time or distance. Only hold your breath for as much as comfortable. Trying to beat yourself will have an adverse effect anyway. You're much better off staying relaxed and seeing where you "pop-up".
- If you begin to panic at any moment, relax and surface.
- Listen to your body. If you get light headed, your vision begins to fade, or you get any other abnormal sensation, surface immediately.

- Work on your lung capacity on dry land and concentrate more on efficient stroke when you're in the water.

Stage 1 - Dry Land Breath Holding

Practice holding your breath for longer periods of time while on dry land.

In the Survival Fitness Plan, we use minimal preparation for breath holding. This is so you know how far you can get in emergency situations. Breathe in, breathe out, breathe in, then go.

Take these breaths slowly from deep within your diaphragm. This is to rid your lungs of low-quality air (CO_2).

Tip: You know you're using correct breathing if your belly is moving up and down rather than your shoulders. When your chest and shoulders move it means you're breathing with only the top part of your lungs. This deep breathing is also useful for recovery after a workout.

Here are more detailed instructions for the inhale, exhale, inhale, sequence.

Whilst doing the following, relax your muscles and remain as still and as calm as possible. This includes not "clock watching" which will make you anxious. The more relaxed and still you are, the less oxygen your body will consume.

- Breathe in for a count of 5 seconds, hold it for 1 second, then breathe out for a count of 10 seconds.
- When exhaling, push out every last drop of air, and push your tongue up against your teeth. This forms a valve which helps to control the release of air. Your breath should make a hissing sound as you exhale.
- Inhale slowly to about 80-85% capacity. Start at the bottom near your diaphragm, then up into your sternum, and finally into your chest.

- Hold your breath for as long as you can, and when you first start to feel the need to breathe, swallow a little spit. This helps to relax your breathing reflex.
- When you need to breathe out, let out little puffs of air at a time.
- When you're finished, push out as much air as possible to get rid of any extra carbon dioxide.

Don't try this sequence again until you get your body back to normal oxygen levels. Breathe steadily for at least 5 minutes and don't do it more than 3 times in a single session. Only do one session a day.

After a few practice sessions try adding in slow movements, such as walking. This will prepare your body to dive and swim with less air.

Stage 2 - Static Underwater Breath Holding

Stage two is the same as stage one, but underwater. The point of this stage is to get you comfortable holding your breath underwater.

Inhale, exhale fully, inhale to 80% capacity, then hold and submerge.

Keep your mouth and nose closed while underwater. Use your fingers to hold your nose shut if you need.

Stay relaxed, and once you are near your limit, resurface. Blow out any extra air as you rise so that you can take a fresh breath immediately.

Stage 3 - Static Apnea Training

In this stage, you will use static apnea training. This conditions your lungs and body to withstand the effects of prolonged breath-holding.

This stage is ongoing. You can move on to stage 4 while doing it.

IMPORTANT: This is a dry land activity. DO NOT try it underwater!

There are two separate programs for static apnea training. One conditions your CO2 tolerance. The other increases the amount of oxygen your lungs can store.

Each program has its own training table. The recovery stage is when you can breathe — breath normal for the allocated time. During the breath hold stage, hold your breath for the allocated time.

Only start O2 tolerance training once you can hold your breath for at least 90 seconds.

You can do both CO2 and O2 sessions on the same day, but do not do them immediately after one another. Do one in the morning and one at night.

Do not do more than one training session of each per day.

CO2 Tolerance

CO2 tolerance training consists of a series of alternating breath-holds and rest periods. Your breathing time gets less and less while your breath holding stays the same.

Start off with a breath-hold period that you're comfortable with. 50-70% of your capability is good. Add 5 or 10 seconds each day.

This table represents one training session, i.e., you recover and breath hold 8 times.

Use the same breath hold time for each one.

In your next training session (the following day), you increase your breath hold time by 5 or 10 seconds.

#	Recovery	Breath Hold
1	2m 30s	50-70%
2	2m 15s	50-70%
3	2m	50-70%
4	1m 45s	50-70%
5	1m 30s	50-70%
6	1m 15s	50-70%
7	1m	50-70%
8	45s	50-70%

O2 Tolerance

In O2 tolerance training, your recovery period stays the same. Instead, you increase your breath holding.

Only start O2 tolerance training once you can hold your breath for at least 90 seconds.

This table represents one training session.

#	Recovery	Breath Hold
1	2m	50%
2	2m	55%
3	2m	60%
4	2m	65%
5	2m	70%
6	2m	75%
7	2m	80%
8	2m	85%

Additional Ways to Increase your Breath Holding Ability

There are some other things you can do to increase your breath holding ability:

- Exercise often.
- Lose weight (if you are overweight).
- Learn to play a wind or brass instrument.
- Take up singing.
- Don't do drugs, especially smoking!

Body Response Information

Important! This is for informational purposes. **DO NOT** *practice/experiment with it.*

When you hold your breath for an extended period of time your body goes through three response stages.

1. **Convulsions.** When you first get an urge to take a breath and you don't, you will have convulsions in your diaphragm. You can learn to fight through this, and if you do then you will gain a couple of minutes before you need to breathe.
2. **Spleen Release.** If you fight through the convulsions your spleen responds by releasing oxygen-rich blood. Your body will calm down and you will get a surge of energy. Use this energy to get somewhere that you can breathe!
3. **Blackout.** If you do not find fresh oxygen you will black out, and if you are underwater at the time you will drown.

Stage 4 - Efficient Stroke

This teaches the technique for an efficient underwater stroke. The only aim is to learn the stroke. Don't try to break any underwater distance records.

This stroke uses a combination of a modified breast-stroke (for the arms) and the dolphin kick. Do it as one fluid motion.

Start off in a streamlined glide and stay in it for as long as possible.

When you are almost to a complete stop, turn your palms out and separate your hands. Do the out-sweep of the breast-stroke. Use webbed finger as described in the freestyle chapter (under the heading Catch). Allow your legs to float up, the higher the better. Keep your head down.

As you do the breaststroke arm movement, arch your body extending your back and shoulders. You aim is to make your body like a spring which you will snap down to propel you forward.

Bring your arms and forearms into a vertical position, elbows facing up. Snap your arms and legs down together.

Your legs/torso do a dolphin kick. Your arms go into a double arm pull stroke by pushing against the water down along your body. Remember your webbed fingers.

Keep your arms vertical for as long as you can and end in a stream-line position with your arms by your sides. Glide in this position for as long as you can.

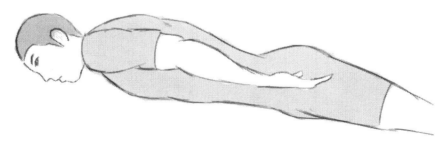

Do a standard breaststroke frog kick. At the same time bring your hands back into the streamline glide you started in, with your arms/hands in front of you.

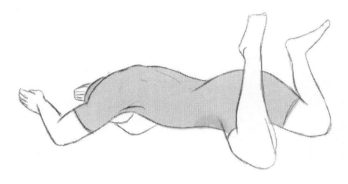

Repeat this sequence. When you start to run out of breath go into your preferred surface stroke. CSS or freestyle is best.

Stage 5 - 50m Swim: Revise the safety pointers from the start of this chapter!

Before attempting this final stage, you should be able to:

- Swim 25 meters underwater in under 30 seconds and using 5 strokes or less.
- Hold your breath for at least 90 seconds while walking on dry land.

The first part of stage 5 is to build up your breath holding ability while moving on dry land.

Hold your breath while doing SFP Super-Burpees for a minute. When you can do 6 in a minute you are ready to attempt the 50-meter underwater swim.

SWIMMING IN OPEN WATER

Being near any body of water has its inherent dangers, and open water has even more. This section gives techniques for swimming in different forms of open water.

In this manual, the term "open water" refers to any natural body of water such as oceans, lakes, and rivers.

PROTECTIVE CLOTHING

Protect yourself from cold and injuries with the appropriate clothing.

Keeping Warm

Being hot outside does not mean it will be warm in the water. It only takes a slight change of weather to take the situation from fun to dangerous.

- Be prepared with the right clothing and use layering.
- Choose fabrics that provide warmth even when wet. Not cotton or jeans.
- In colder conditions, use a wetsuit.
- Once out of the water, put on warm clothes. Use clothing that blocks the wind, such as a poncho.

Layering

Layering means using several items of thin clothing as opposed to one or two thick ones. If you get too warm you can strip one or two layers without losing all your protection.

There are three basic layers. Base, insulator and outer.

Base Layer

The first layer, (base layer), will reduce water flowing past your skin and is also good for sun protection. You want a skin-tight, quick-drying material that will wick the water away. Rash vests are a good example. Polypropylene, polyester, and lycra are good materials for your base layer.

Insulating Layer

The insulating layer keeps you warm when it gets colder. It should fit snug. Not too tight or too loose. Use materials that dry fast. Unlined tracksuits work well, as does wool and fleece. Unlined is important, otherwise, it will hold air and water. A hooded top helps to prevent heat from escaping through your head. It also provides sun protection.

Adjust the number of insulating layers you use depending on the temperature. In warmer climates, you may not even need one.

Outer Layer

Your outer layer should be a water and windproof shell. Its purpose is to keep you warm and the elements (such as wind and rain) out. You will still get wet, either from perspiration or from being in the water.

A rain jacket, an anorak or a light nylon over-all works well. It should be large enough so you have good freedom of movement. This will also trap a warm layer of air inside it.

Being windproof is very important for the outer layer.

Other Considerations: Footwear

Footwear is especially important in unknown waters where your feet may get injured. Simple canvas shoes with drain holes work well. Wear ones that are easy to remove in case you get caught in rocks.

Wearing socks provides insulation and also prevents chafing.

Swimming in footwear, as with any clothing, will create extra drag. Experiment with it during training.

Goggles

Swimming goggles, or a mask, are not essential but are useful if you want to see underwater.

It is a good idea to always wear goggles in a chlorinated/chemical pool.

Poncho

A poncho is an excellent all-around piece of survival equipment. When it comes to water training, you will use ponchos for some self-rescue exercises. It can also become an improvised shelter or emergency blanket (extra warmth) when not in the water.

Visibility

Being visible in the water is for safety and survival. You want to be easy to spot by any water traffic. Also, if you get in trouble you will be easier to find by rescue services.

Maintenance

Always wash yourself and all your gear in fresh water after training in any type of water. This will keep everything in the best working condition for as long as possible.

Rinsing your gear under a tap is not enough. Most of the bad stuff (salt, chemicals, etc.) will not get washed out. It is best to wear it in the shower or put it in the washing machine.

Restrictions

The more clothes you have on the harder it will be to swim. The best way to prepare is to simulate falling into the water while clothed and then swimming to safety.

Water-logged clothes will also make climbing out of the water harder.

SAFE ENTRY TECHNIQUES

There are a variety of ways to enter the water. The methods described in this section focus on safety and are also used in rescue situations.

Always enter shallow or unknown waters feet first. Unknown waters are when you are unsure of the water depth, and/or if you can't see what lays beneath the surface.

Wade Entry

When possible, the wade entry is the best way to enter unknown waters.

It is walking into the water very carefully. Feel your way forward with your feet until the water is chest deep, then start to swim.

Slide Entry

Use the slide entry for shallow or unknown waters with a steep angled edge, such as a pool edge. It is also useful in crowded areas since it is easier to control than other entry methods.

The slide entry is very simple. Sit down with your feet/legs hanging down into (or above) the water. Use your hands to slide yourself into the water.

For shallow waters, once your feet are firm, continue forward using the wade entry.

If speed is a factor and you plan to push off the wall once you are in the water, don't push too hard during the slide entry. If you are too far away from the edge you won't be able to do a good push off, which is where your initial propulsion comes from.

Step-off Entry

When entering shallow or unknown waters, and you are too high for a slide entry, use the step-off.

Step off your platform into the water. Keep your knees flexed and be ready to absorb any impact in case you hit the floor.

You can then wade or swim depending on the situation.

Stride Entry

Only use the stride entry when you know the water is at least 1.5 meters deep, and the slide entry is not appropriate.

One of the big advantages of the stride entry is that you keep your head above the water. This means you can keep your sight on something, such as a drowning victim.

Put your arms out to your sides and step one foot out in front of you. Planted your foot well so you don't slip. Keep looking at your target the whole time.

Look up a little as you lean forward into the water.

Slap your hands down as you hit the water. Looking up and slapping down helps to keep your head above the water.

High-Level Entry

This is good to use when you have to enter the water from a height of 3+ meters. You must be sure that the water depth is appropriate for the height you are jumping from. Also ensure that your landing zone is a large enough area-wise, i.e., length and width.

Unlike all the previous entry methods, the high-level entry is not safe to do while carrying gear. If you have a backpack or anything else, throw it in before jumping.

Consider wearing long clothing as it will help protect your body.

Take a large breath and jump away from the surface. You don't want to hit anything on the way down.

Cross your ankles and place your hands in fists in front of your thighs. This puts your arms down and close to your body.

Bend your knees a little.

Look straight ahead at the horizon and arch your back. Looking down or up will cause you to lean forward or back respectively. Arching your back will help keep you straight. You want to hit the water as vertical and straight as possible.

Allow your knees to flex once you hit the water. This will help slow you down.

Height vs Water Depth

The higher your jumping-off platform, the deeper the water needs to be.

The best way to judge is if you have seen others do it, and even then you must be very careful.

Note: All these calculations are only approximate so it is easy to do them in your head. The results are good enough to use.

Start with at least 2.5 meters (m) of water depth. If you're jumping from higher than 1.5 m you need to add an extra 0.6 m of depth for every 3 m increase in height.

Calculating Height

A simple but effective way to calculate your height from the water is to drop something into it. Any solid object that won't catch air will work, like a rock. Time how long it takes to hit the water.

Multiply that number by itself, and then multiply that answer by 16, i.e., (x^2) x 16.

This gives you the approximate height in feet. Multiply it by 0.3 to convert it into meters.

Calculating Water Depth

Get a long stick (or something similar) and put it in the water until it hits the floor. Measure how much of it got wet.

This is easy in theory but hard in practice.

SURVIVAL SWIMMING STYLES

In order to successfully overcome obstacles in the water you need to adjust your swimming style depending on the situation and what lays ahead.

The Defensive Position

In most cases, the best thing to do when experiencing trouble in the water is to tread water and signal for help. When in swift water treading may not be practical as the current will drag you away.

In this case, the best thing to do is adopt the defensive position.

Get on your back with your feet up so you can see your toes. Float downstream feet first.

This position will enable you to see the path ahead. Guide yourself through the safest route of passage.

If you meet any obstructions, absorb the impact with your legs.

Keeping your feet up ensures they don't get caught in obstructions beneath the surface.

Never try to stand up in river rapids that are deep enough for you to float in.

When you see an obstruction you want to avoid, angle your body so that your feet point towards the obstacle. Aim the top of your head towards your destination and use a modified sculling motion to get there.

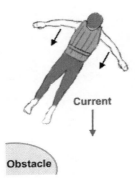

The Aggressive Position

If you see an opportunity to get to safety, and it is deep enough to do so, you can use an aggressive position to get there. The aggressive position is doing freestyle while keeping your head out of the water.

The aggressive position is very tiring so reserve it for when you need short bursts of power. You could also use breast or side stroke. They will be slower but with better visibility.

WAVES

By being able to identify the types of waves you can make the best decision about whether it is safe to swim in them or not. There are three basic types of waves to look for. Spilling, plunging, and surging.

Spilling Waves

A spilling wave is when the crest of the wave tumbles down its front. If the sandbank it breaks on is shallow it will form a "tube".

Spilling waves occur on ocean floors with a gradual slope. They are most common with onshore winds (winds that blow across the ocean towards land). They break for longer and in a gentle fashion when compared to other waves.

They are the safest types of waves to swim in.

Plunging Waves

Plunging waves occur when the beach slope is moderate to steep or if it has a sudden change in depth, e.g., a reef or sandbar. They usually occur with offshore winds (winds that blow across the land towards the ocean) and at low tide.

These waves become more vertical than spilling waves and break with much more force. Experienced surfers often enjoy them for the "tube" they may create.

Plunging waves have a lot more potential to cause serious injury to the swimmer. It is best to not swim in them.

If caught in a plunging wave, hug your knees and roll up into a ball.

Surging Waves

Surging waves occur when long period swells meet steep beach slopes. The bottom of the wave is fast enough that the crest never forms. As a result, there is little sign of breaking/whitewash.

Surging waves are dangerous. Although the wave break is minimal, the force of the wave is still powerful. They can knock you over and then drag you out to sea.

Do not to swim when there are surging waves.

Although not waves, another thing to be aware of is rough or choppy water. Rough seas can quickly drain your energy. It is best to get out and wait until the water is calm again.

Riding Waves to Shore

When the waves are not too large you can use them to carry you to shore. Choose your wave and swim forward with it. Before it breaks dive down a little so the break goes over you.

Large Waves

With larger surf, it is better to swim towards shore between oncoming waves. As a wave approaches, face it and go under water until it has passed over you. Swim towards the shore as much as you can before repeating the process with the next wave.

You may get caught in the undertow of a large wave. Get to the surface to avoid getting dragged out too far.

Rocky Shores

Only try to land on rocky shores if there is no other option. It is better to do a long distance swim to an easier landing point than it is to risk injury on rocky shores.

When you have to land on a rocky shore you must choose a safe landing point. Avoid where the waves crash into the rocks with a high white spray. Instead, aim for where the waves rush up onto rocks.

Once you know where you want to land, approach slowly. Use a large wave to carry you in. Get into the defensive position so you can absorb the impact.

If you do not reach the shore on the first wave, swim in the aggressive position with your hands only. When the next wave approaches, re-adopt the defensive position.

When you climb up the rocks keep your knees a little bent and your feet close together.

CURRENTS

Current refers to the constant flow of water. It is always there and it acts differently depending on many factors. These include water volume, channel width, gradient, weather, obstructions, etc.

Although you can use water currents in your favor, they can also take you where you do not want to go. Even slow ones can knock a person off his feet and carry him out to sea/downstream.

Currents are usually slower along the inside bend of rivers opposed to the outside bend. Also, currents are faster on the surface of the water.

Rip Currents

Rip currents can occur near beaches with breaking waves. They are strong currents which drag swimmers out to sea. Generally, the larger the waves, the stronger the rip current will be.

Signs of a Rip Current

The following characteristics can indicate a rip current:

- A channel of rippled water (more-so than the surrounding water)
- Dark water (indicates greater depth)
- Debris and/or sea-foam moving in a steady line out to sea.
- Different colored water beyond the breaking waves.
- Murky water (indicates disturbed sand by the rip)
- Waves breaking further out to sea on both sides of the rip.

Look for a channel of water that is different (calmer or choppier) than the water surrounding it.

A rip current may also be present with none of these characteristics showing.

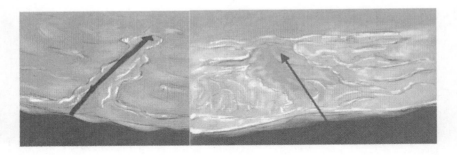

Escaping the Rip Current

- Do not try to swim against it!
- Stay calm
- Swim parallel to the shore until you reach the breaking waves zone, then swim back to shore.
- If you can't escape it, conserve your energy (float or tread water) and signal for help.

In this picture, the thin arrows show the direction of the current. The 4 thicker arrows are your channels of escape.

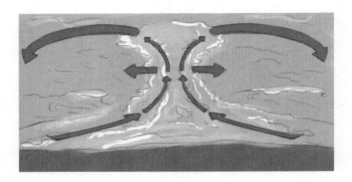

River Current

When swimming across a river you must allow for the drag of the current. Choose your exit point and then choose an entry point upstream. How far upstream you need to enter depends on the strength of the current and how strong of a swimmer you are. Use your best judgment.

Use the aggressive swimming technique (freestyle with your head above water).

When there is more than one swimmer it is a good idea to pair (or triple if there is an odd number) them up. Pair a good swimmer that knows proper rescue techniques with a weak one so he can help if needed.

Improvised Flotation Aids

Any medium-sized object that floats can aid you when swimming across a body of water. A football, styrofoam cooler, floating log, etc.

Lashing together smaller empty containers also works well in slow water.

Tie your flotation device to your wrist and grab onto it if you get tired. You could also hug it with one arm although you would need to improvise your stroke. Sidestroke would work well for this.

Inflating Your Clothes

Being stranded in the water and having to tread water to stay afloat expends precious energy. When you are wearing long clothes you can trap air inside them to help you float.

These methods work best with waterproof materials. For cotton clothing, keep the material that is out of the water wet to prevent air escaping.

Inflating Your Top

As you tread water (feet only), pull up your collar and bunch your shirt around your mouth to make a tight seal. Keep your nose out in the open.

Breathe in through your nose and exhale out your mouth into your shirt. Direct air into your shoulder area by leaning forward.

Inflating Your Trousers

If you cannot take your trousers off over your shoes, remove them. Tie the laces together, and then hang them around your neck.

Remove your pants, do the zip up, and tie the bottom of the trouser legs together.

Inflate your trouser legs using either the blow, sling, or splash method.

After inflating your pants keep the waistband underwater. Put your head between the legs and hug the pants with the fly facing your body. Fold or twist the waistband closed to create a seal. You can rest your head back on the knot.

Keep the exposed material wet by splashing water on it.

When needed, open the waistband (while keeping it underwater) and scoop more air in.

Blow Method

This method is best for weak swimmers.

Hold the pants the right way up by the waistband, with the fly facing you. Take a deep breath and go underwater with the pants. Blow air into them.

Keeping the pants underwater, take another breath and blow more air into them. Repeat this until they filled with air.

Sling Method

Hold the trousers behind your head by the waistband ensuring you keep it open. Using a forceful motion, sling the pants over your head in front of you and into the water to fill them with air.

Splash Method

Hold the waistband open underwater with one hand, fly facing up and trousers on the surface. Use your other hand inside the waistband to scoop water and air bubbles into your trousers. Scoop fast. The water will pass through leaving the air trapped.

OBSTRUCTIONS

An obstruction is anything in the water which changes the normal flow (current) of the water. Almost anything in the water will do this, such as rocks, branches, etc.

There are specific techniques to use depending on the obstruction you come across.

Drops

A drop is when water drops straight down. A waterfall is an obvious example.

Never go in the water upstream from a drop. Even if the water is shallow and appears calm before the drop, it is still very dangerous.

When going over a drop is unavoidable, ball up and try to land feet first. Landing feet first is best to protect your head. Balling up will lessen the possibility of getting caught in a foot entrapment.

If it is a high drop, as you go over the edge adopt the high-level entry position.

Eddies

Eddies occur when water rushes around obstacles and the current comes back on itself. They are often a safe-haven since the water in the eddy is generally calmer.

The barrier of separation between the upstream and downstream water is the eddy line. Problems can occur when crossing this line, especially if the flow is fast. Unless you are in a craft that can capsize (like a kayak) you shouldn't face much danger.

You can break through the eddy line with barrel rolls.

As you approach the eddy, place your closest hand into the upstream moving water inside it.

Scoop the water with this hand as you roll over onto your stomach. You are now in the aggressive swimming position.

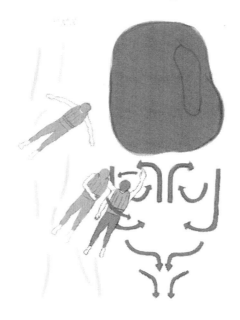

Continue to roll until you are back in the defensive swimming position.

You may need to barrel roll a few times to get into the eddy. You can finish in either the defensive or aggressive swimming position.

This image is a demonstration of using defensive and aggressive swimming to get out of a river.

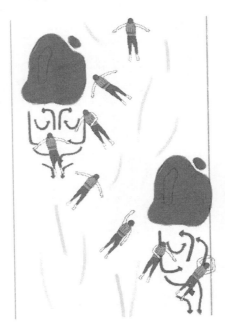

Sometimes an eddy can create a whirlpool effect. This is when eddies become dangerous since the whirlpool can suck you down. In this case, you should stay clear of them.

Entrapments

An entrapment is anything that you can get snagged on, e.g., your clothing snagging on a branch underwater.

To prevent this, make sure all your gear and clothing is a snug fit.

A foot entrapment is when you get your foot stuck. It is very dangerous as the force of the water can hold you under.

Holes

Holes occur when water flows over a ledge (such as a rock). This creates a hydraulic flow (water circulating on top of itself) which can trap things. It is like a vertical eddy and is very dangerous.

Dams and dam-like structures (weirs, spillways, ledges) have severe hydraulic action. Keep away from their downstream base.

If caught in a hole you need to relax and swim out the bottom (where the slower current flows out) or to the side.

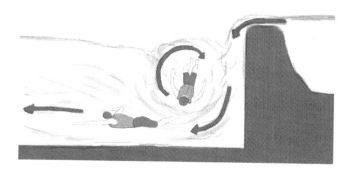

Pillows

When a rock is close to the waters surface the water hits the top of it, forcing it upwards. This creates a "pillow" of water downstream of the rock.

The more submerged a rock is, the further downstream the pillow will be. If the rock is very close to the surface the pillow will be right on top of it. With enough experience, you will be able to tell when a rock is close to the surface or not by the type of pillow it creates.

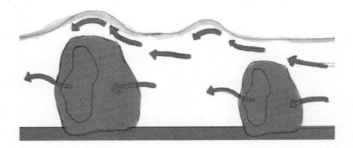

If the rock is out of the water, the pillow becomes a cushion. This is due to the water flowing up against it. When the current is strong enough, it may form a series of compression waves.

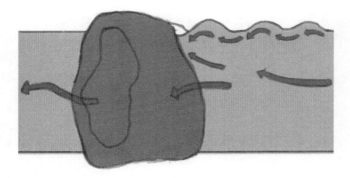

Rapids

A rapid is a turbulent section of water created by faster flowing water over obstacles, such as rocks. These obstacles may or may not break the water's surface. This faster water is due to an increased gradient and/or a constriction in the channel.

To negotiate a rapid, look for a downstream "V" in the water (the bottom of the V pointing downstream). This indicates an unobstructed flow of water. In most cases, it will be the preferred path of passage.

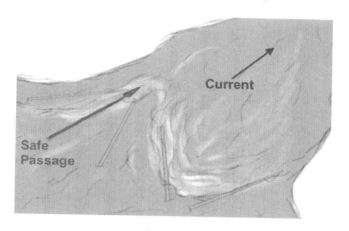

Rocks

Apart from being a cause for other types of obstructions, the rock itself can present danger. Avoid these obstructions altogether by entering the water downstream of them.

Walking on slippery rocks (or any slippery surface) near water is never a good idea.

Rocks under the water's surface can become foot entrapments. It is very dangerous and is one of the main reasons to keep your feet up in the defensive position.

When in the water heading towards a rock, use the defensive position as described before.

If you get pinned up against a rock, lean downstream to get loose.

Rocks are not all bad. They may serve as a lifeline to hold onto. They can also create eddies which can be safe havens in turbulent waters.

Sweepers and Strainers

Strainers are objects in the water that allow water to pass through them but not objects. They can be natural like branches, or artificial such as wire fences.

A sweeper is a strainer that hangs low over or into the water.

Both of these things can impede your safe passage, and they often double as entrapments.

When swimming into a strainer is unavoidable, maneuver into the aggressive swimming position. Swim hard to launch yourself up and onto (or over) the obstruction.

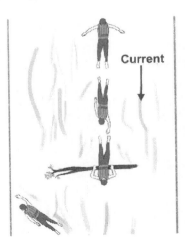

When forced below the surface swim downstream using your hands in front of you to part the branches.

If your legs get tangled in long weeds swim downstream using only your arms.

Like friendly rocks, sometimes sweepers (not strainers) can serve as a lifeline. You might be able to use them to climb to shore.

Undercut Rocks

An undercut rock is one where the water flows below it as opposed to around. The water's current can drag the swimmer underneath it and pin him there.

Normal river features acting strangely are good indications of an undercut rock, e.g.,

- The pillow or cushion is missing
- There is a boil (where the water is not flowing down or upstream) on the downstream side of the obstacle.
- The eddy has weak (or missing) lines and/or an abnormal current flow.

Water Debris

Water debris is anything floating in the water. It can be either natural or unnatural, such as seaweed, logs, trash, etc.

Keep an eye out for these things and avoid them as they can become entrapments.

If there is a lot of debris, such as lots of seaweed, try to avoid it. If you must go through it then crawl over the top by grasping at it with over-hand movements. When you are in a group put the strongest person first. He will create a path through the debris for the others to follow.

Manmade pools created behind dams often have many stumps lying below the surface. This is due to the cutting of trees before the flooding of the lowlands.

People

Other people can be a hazard, although more often they are a good thing in a survival situation.

When in open water there are more recreational hazards. Surfers, jet-skis, boats, etc. Stay away from areas in which these activities take place. If available, use the designated swimming areas instead.

Pollution

Another by-product of people is pollution. Water systems are often used as a dumping ground for all sorts of human and industrial waste.

Swimming in polluted waters may not have an immediate effect, but it could result in illness later.

LEARN TO SWIM

This is the original Survival Swimming book. It is for people learning how to swim and teaches basic skills and strokes.

CONQUERING THE FEAR OF WATER

People are usually only afraid of water because they are not used to it. The following exercises will allow the user to gradually build confidence in the water.

Do these exercises in shallow water.

Enjoy Water

Sit on the pool edge with your legs dangling in the water.

Move them back and forth and enjoy the water flowing around your legs.

Splash your face.

Walk around in the water.

Submerge Your Head

Hold your breath and crouch down until your head is under water. When you need to breathe, stand up.

Bob up and down in the water. Submerge your head with each bob down.

Blowing Bubbles

Hold your breath and crouch down so that your mouth is below the water surface but your nose is not.

Slowly exhale through your mouth, blowing bubbles in the water.

Crouch lower so that only your eyes are not submerged. Now blow bubbles through your nose and mouth.

Lastly, put your whole head underwater and blow bubbles.

Floating: Mushroom Float

Hold your breath and curl up by drawing your knees to your chest.

Hold onto your knees or ankles and float.

Horizontal Glide

Hold your breath and push off the wall with your legs.

Extend your arms forward at the same time.

Extend your body to get as horizontal as you can.

Your head is in line with your trunk.

Exhale as you glide.

FLUTTER KICK

The flutter kick is a basic propulsion technique mainly used when doing freestyle (a.k.a. over arm, front crawl).

Grab the edge of the pool, arms extended. Alternately kick up and down with your legs, toes pointed.

Kick from the hips. Be relaxed and compact. Get your body straight and horizontal. Put your head in the water in line with your body.

Get to the point where you only hold onto the edge with your finger-tips, then release your hold.

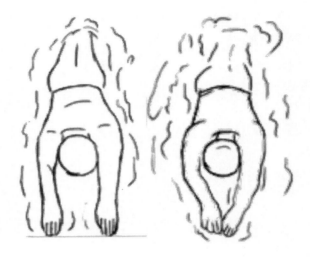

If your hips and legs drop, increase the downward pressure on your head and chest.

Next, hold a kick-board with extended arms in front of you.

Do the flutter kick.

Lift your head to breathe in then put it back into the water to breathe out.

Finally, do it without the kick board.

BREASTSTROKE KICK
a.k.a. Frog Kick

The breast stroke kick can be hard to master, but this set of exercises will show you how to get maximum propulsion.

Standing Individual Leg Kick

Stand upright with both feet close together and arms at your sides. Do the following with one leg.

Recovery

Flex your foot towards your shin (dorsi-flexion) and bring your heel towards your buttocks.

Catch

When your foot is close to your buttocks, raise your leg sideways while keeping your knee bent and your foot in dorsi-flexion.

Out-sweep

When you have raised your leg about 45°, extend your leg and point your foot/toes (plantar flexion).

Keep your leg lifted sideways.

In-sweep

Bring your leg back into the initial position at the end of the leg extension.

Practice until it is a fluid motion.

Breaststroke Kick on a Chair

Sit towards the front of the chair and grab the sides for support.

Extend your legs forward, and lift them about 5 inches above the ground.

Point your feet and do the kick with both feet simultaneously.

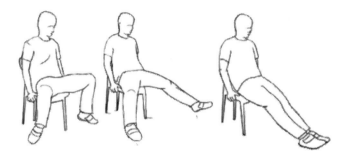

Breaststroke Kick on the Floor

Lie on your stomach with your arms comfortably in front of you. Practice the kick.

Breaststroke Kick on Pool Edge

Lie on the edge of the pool with your upper body resting on the wall and your legs in the water. Practice the kick.

With Floating Aids

Use one or more water noodles to keep you floating with your shoulders and head above water.

Get on your stomach with your arms extended forward.

Push off the ground and use the breaststroke kick for propulsion.

Keep your head above water.

Do the same again but with a kick-board held at arms' length.

Now incorporate breathing. Just before you recover your feet towards the buttocks, raise your head and inhale.

Let your chest and head drop back into the water after breathing and immediately start to exhale.

Your legs continue the recovery.

DOGGY PADDLE

Use doggy paddle when clothed or wearing a life jacket.

Although slow in speed, it requires very little energy over short distances and your head stays above water.

With your stomach face down, look forwards with your head above the water.

Use the flutter kick.

Extend your arms in front of you, palms turned downward.

Keep your arms underwater and alternatively move each arm forward until it is fully extended.

Your arm continues to down and backward until it arrives at the level of your chest.

Repeat this in a continuous circular motion.

ELEMENTARY BACKSTROKE

Use it if an underwater explosion is likely or if you are tired from other strokes.

Head Lead Supine Balance

Lie flat on your back and contract your abs to keep a straight back.

Your head is in line with your trunk and your chin is tucked a little.

Keep your arms relaxed and extended at your sides and use a gentle flutter kick.

If your hips and legs drop increase the downward pressure on your shoulder blades and on the back of your head.

Swimming Elementary Backstroke

Glide on your back.

Your head is in line with your trunk and your face is out of the water.

Inhale and draw your hands up towards your armpits, bending at your elbows.

At the same time, bring your feet to your bum. Keep your legs together.

Now exhale.

Extend your arms sideways to form a T with your body. Your palms face backwards. Spread your legs apart while keeping them bent.

Sweep your arms backwards and inwards to be brought back to your sides simultaneously.

At the same time extend your legs backwards then squeeze them together once they are fully extended in their original position.

Glide for a bit then repeat.

FREESTYLE
a.k.a. Front Crawl, Over-arm

The freestyle stroke is fast and efficient.

Head Lead Prone Balance

Lie flat in the water, face down.

Keep your head in line with your trunk.

Your arms are relaxed along the sides of your body.

Use a flutter kick.

When you need to breathe, gently extend your chin forward to bring your mouth out of the water.

As you do so, apply downward pressure on your chest and head.

Head Lead Side Balance

Do the head-lead supine balance as previously described, and then roll on your side so that your top arm and a bit of the top of your thigh are out of the water.

Use a flutter kick.

Do not move your head while you roll on the side.

Roll as far as possible while keeping on your side.

Apply downward pressure on your bottom shoulder.

Head-Lead Nose Up/Nose Down

Start with the head lead side balance.

Roll your head downward to look at the bottom of the pool.

Let your body roll until it is at a 90° angle from the surface.

Slowly exhale through your nose and mouth.

When you need to breathe, roll back.

Roll between the upward and downward position.

Head Lead Looking Down

Start in head lead side balance and roll into the nose down position.

Use your kick and continue to roll until you are floating on the other side of your body.

Roll your body as a unit.

Take a few breaths then roll back the other way.

Hand Lead Side Balance

Start in the head lead side balance then extend your bottom arm under water so it is straight in an overhead position. Your arm is parallel to the water surface or slightly angled down. Experiment with arm and hand position to discover what's most comfortable.

Note: You move faster with an arm extended.

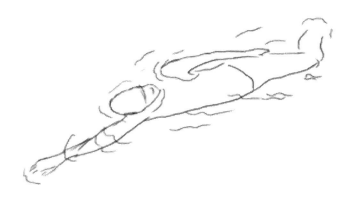

Hand Lead Nose Up Nose Down

From the hand lead side balance, rotate your head down to look at the bottom of the pool.

Your body follows to roll on the side so it is at a 90° angle with the surface.

When you need to, roll in the upward position, take a few breaths, and then roll down again.

Under Switch

Adopt the hand lead nose down position.

Your top arm is the recovering arm. Bring it forward in the water and close to your body.

Your hand follows the mid-line of your body with your palm turned inward.

At the same time, sweep backward with your other arm.

When you see your recovering hand in front of your face, roll your body to the other side.

Next, do double and triple switches by doing a few arm switches before rolling up. Snap your hip rotation.

Zipper Switch

Start as you did in the under switch.

Sweep your hand past your hip, rib cage and shoulder, as if pulling up a zipper.

Use a high elbow and let your forearm dangle with your hand dragging in the water.

Once your hand has moved past your head, put your arm in the water and extend it forward into the overhead position.

As your recovering arm enters the water, the other arm starts to sweep backward.

Simultaneously roll on your other side and continue the arm movements until one arm is completely extended in the overhead position and the other arm rests on your top side.

You are now on your other side.

Take a few breathes and then repeat.

When comfortable, do multiple switches.

Over Switch

Get into hand lead nose down and start the recovery forward with your top arm, leading with the elbow.

Your recovering hand hovers closely above the water surface.

As your hand passes your head, swipe your thumb/inner side of your hand across the side of your head at your temple.

Put your arm into the water in front of your head right after the swipe and extend your arm forward under water until it is fully extended.

Just as your recovering arm enters the water, your other arm starts to sweep backward in the water.

Roll your body on the side of your recovering arm as it extends forward.

Also, roll your head up until you are in the hand lead side balance position.

When comfortable do multiple switches.

Swimming Free Style

Do multiple over switches but leave out the thumb swipe.

Angle your hand down when entering the water, and then bring it parallel to the surface midway through the underwater recovery.

Finally, angle it up when the arm is completely extended.

When recovering, your hand enters the water midway between your head and your hand once your arm is extended.

Do not to extend your arm forward underwater at the end of the recovery.

Every third arm stroke, inhale.

Only roll as far as needed for your mouth to clear the water.

Exhale as soon as your head rolls downward and exhale continuously until your head rolls upward to catch the next breath.

To breathe, roll on your side and let your head roll a little bit further until your mouth clears the water.

Swim more on your sides rather than flat on your stomach and chest.

Roll from side to side with each arm stroke.

Keep your elbow high in the water during the underwater arm pull.

Use a two-beat kick for middle and long distance swimming i.e. kick at the same pace as you stroke with your arms.

BREAST STROKE

Use this stroke to swim underwater, through oil or debris, or in rough seas. It is also good for long-range swimming. It is slower than freestyle but uses less energy.

Practice your arm movement standing on dry land.

Glide

Your arms are straight and extended overhead.

Keep your hands close together and your palms faced down.

Out Sweep

Separate your hands and move your arms outwards until they are outside the shoulders.

Your palms face either downwards or slightly outwards.

Catch

Bend your arms at the elbows and move your forearms down and backwards.

Keep your hands in line with your forearms and your shoulders close to the water surface.

Keep moving your arms in this fashion until your forearms and palms are facing backwards.

In Sweep

Move your forearms backwards and inwards whilst facing them backwards for as long as possible.

Continue to move your arms until your hands are close together below your chest.

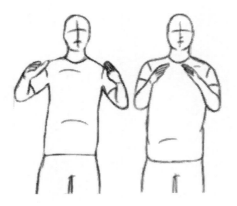

Recovery

Move your arms quickly forward in a straight line until they are completely extended, with your hands close together.

Your forearms and palms rotate outwards until they face down into the glide position.

Once you are confident, practice in the water.

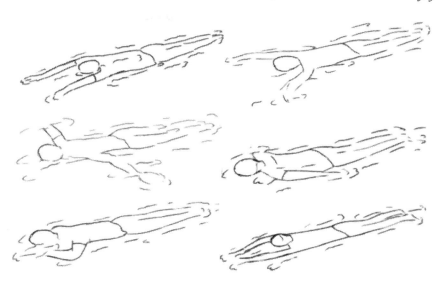

Breathing

During the in sweep, your head and shoulders rise above the water for you to breathe in.

During the arm recovery forward your head and shoulders drop back into the water.

Exhale until the next in sweep.

Co-ordination of Arms and Legs

Get into the glide position with a water noodle across your chest and under your armpits.

Start the arm stroke cycle.

Start the recovery of the legs towards the buttocks at the end of the arms' in sweep, then catch and sweep out with your legs during the arms' recovery forward.

Your legs continue to sweep out and then to sweep in while your arms are extended forward.

At the end of the kick, glide for a moment.

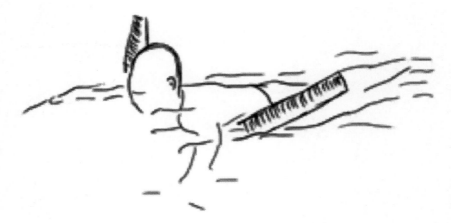

Practice first without breathing and then when comfortable, add in breathing. Finally, remove the noodle.

SIDESTROKE

Sidestroke is good to adopt when you need a break from other strokes i.e. sore muscles, and is also used for rescue.

Dry Land Scissor Kick

Lie on the floor on your left side.

Extend your left arm above your head, palm turned towards the floor.

Your head rests against your extended arm.

Push against the floor with your right hand to maintain balance.

Bend your knees and bring your legs towards your chest until your thighs make a 90° angle with your torso.

Spread your legs, with the upper leg kicking to the front and the lower leg to the back.

Extend your legs, and then bring them back to the initial position.

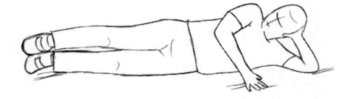

Repeat and practice on both sides.

Dry Land Sidestroke Arms

Stand upright and extend your left arm straight above your head, palm turned to the right.

Your right arm and hand rest at the side of your body.

Your palm is turned towards the body and your head is slightly rotated to the right.

Bend your left elbow and bring your arm down until your hand reaches your chest.

At the same time, bend your right elbow and bring your forearm up until both palms meet in front of your chest.

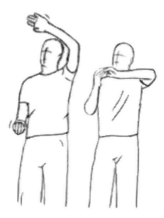

Extend your left arm above your head to the initial position.

At the same time, the palm of the right arm turns downward, the arm straightens back to its initial position and the hand executes a sweeping motion to stroke 'the water'.

Dry Land Sidestroke

To synchronize arms and legs, bring the upper leg towards the chest at the same time as the upper arm moves towards the chest to meet the lower arm.

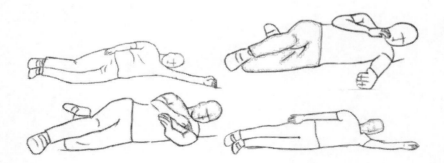

Scissor Kick in Water

Put a water noodle under the arm pit of the side you want to swim on.

Push off the wall and take on the initial position of the sidestroke. Practice the scissor kick.

When comfortable, try without the noodle.

Arm Motion in Water

Put a pull buoy between your legs.

Push off the wall and take on the initial position of the sidestroke.

Practice the arm motions alone.

Swimming Sidestroke

Put a swim noodle under the arm pit of the side on which you will be swimming and swim sidestroke.

Finally, swim without the noodle.

MOUNTAIN BIKE RIDING

Most people know how to ride, but many do not know how to ride fast or through obstacles in a safe manner. This section will teach you how.

BASIC RIDING SKILLS

Braking

Use the brakes together. Pull the rear brake lever first and then gradually squeeze the front as you brace yourself against the handlebars. Too much front brake and you will go over the handle bars (endo), too much rear brake and you will skid out of control.

The more weight over the wheel the more stopping power it will have. Use this to your advantage e.g. leaning back while braking downhill will help to prevent endos.

The faster you are going the longer it will take to slow down. Keep your brakes covered at all times.

Using Gears

Higher gears are harder to pedal and will help you go faster. Lower gears are easier to pedal and help you get up hills. Shift before you get to the hill.

It is better to pedal faster in a low (easy) gear as opposed to slowly in a high gear.

Looking Ahead

As you ride, look ahead so you can adjust to any obstacles. Slow down for blind corners and brake or steer early and smoothly rather than leaving it to the last minute.

BASIC DRILLS

Use the following drills to improve your basic riding skills.

Stand and Coast

Stand on your pedals without sitting on the seat and just coast. Keep your arms bent and don't lock your knees. Put your pedals horizontal i.e. pedals level.

Next, shift your body towards the rear of the bike. Use this position when coasting over obstacles or rough terrain.

Stand and Pedal

Lift yourself off the seat and pedal.

Track Stand

Balance the bicycle in place, keeping your feet on the pedals. Use in case have to move quickly, or to stop short to analyze an obstacle without losing your rhythm.

Coast at a slow speed, pedals level, and then come to a stop. Find your balance position. You can stand, sit, turn your wheel at an angle, etc. Whatever works for you.

Lightly rock back and forth. To rock forward let off the brake a little. To rock back pull the bike back underneath you. Repeat this procedure.

Keep pressure on your front pedal whilst holding the brake to keep you in place.

Slow Ride

Ride between two points as slowly as possible without putting your foot down. Ride forward at all times. No zigzagging etc.

Heel Grab

The goal is to grab onto one of your heels and keep riding along normally.

Pedal normally then lean to your left and use your left hand to grab onto your left heel. Continue to hold your heel as you pedal.

You can start off holding your calf, then move to your ankle, then your heel.

Bottle Pick Up

Ride towards an upright bottle so it is just off to your side. As you ride past the bottle, lean over and pick it up off the ground. Next, place it back on the ground in an upright position.

Slalom

Look straight ahead and weave in and out of a set of obstacles in a zigzag fashion i.e. to the left of the first obstacle, right of the second, left of the third etc. Start with the obstacles in a straight line about 6 feet apart and bring them closer together as you improve.

Offset Slalom

Use the same set-up as with the regular slalom but take every other cone and move it left or right 2-3 feet. You'll have to take wider, sweeping turns and lean more to get around the obstacles. Continue to look ahead.

Figure 8's

Ride your bike in a figure 8 in as small a space as possible without putting your foot down.

Gap Storming

Arrange two lines of cones in a V formation. Ride between them without hitting any. As your confidence increases, move the final pair closer and closer together.

Down A Curb

Coast straight down off a curb. Absorb the drop with your arms and legs.

ADVANCED SKILLS

Fixing a Dropped Chain

If your chain drops onto the bottom bracket just pedal easily and gently shift up with the 'big' gears.

If the chain is jammed get off the bike and manually put it back on.

If the chain falls outside the crank arm e.g. on your foot, then roll and shift down toward the small ring. You can use your foot to help place it back on.

Learning to Crash

Use the roll taught in parkour. Get comfortable doing a forward roll after a running dive. Progress the 'crash' to rolling after slamming on your front brakes when riding on grass.

Cornering

Always look where you want to go. Anticipate the speed for the corner and brake before the corner if necessary. Never brake while turning. Approach the corner wide. Cut to the apex (the straightest line through a corner), and finish wide.

If you stop pedaling, put all your weight onto the outside pedal so it faces down towards the road. Resume peddling as soon as you have passed the apex.

Riding Faster

Push and pull the pedal around as if keeping the pedal to the outside of the circle. Lift your knees faster and higher.

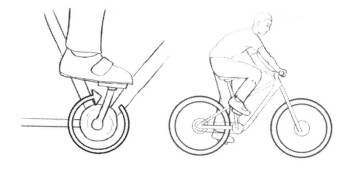

Uphill

If you need to shift during a climb take a couple power strokes first. Soft pedal for a stroke while you shift, then pedal hard again.

On the road you can stand, but on dirt stay seated. Slide your bum forward on your seat, and lean over the handlebars. Put your elbows back (not down). Pedal smooth.

Downhill

To prevent the chain from falling off, shift into the big chain-ring.

Stand with pedals level and shift your weight over the back wheel. Stay loose on the bike. Don't lock your elbows or clench your grip. Steer with your body. Let your shoulders guide you.

Brake on solid dirt or rock where you can get traction, as opposed to loose soil or gravel.

Floating Over Terrain

On rough terrain, let the bike float underneath you. It will move in different directions as it hits bumps. Keep your body upright and the bike pointed down the trail.

Looking Behind

Make sure the path ahead is clear. Relax your right arm to drop your shoulder a little. Your elbow bends and your right hand is relaxed. Turn your head left and slide your butt to the right as you glance over your shoulder.

Down A Ledge

Shift your weight back, drop your wrists to pull up the handlebars and level the bike. Shift your weight forward as the rear wheel goes airborne.

Log Hopping

Get in the same position as if you were riding downhill.

Front Pull

Coast at medium speed and, without braking, push down on the handlebars. Pull upward and straighten your arms to bring the front wheel off the ground. Place it back down gently.

Hip Hop

Shift your weight forward and turn your pedals so that your feet are almost vertical.

Press back against the pedals as you push your legs up.

Pull the back end up with your leg muscles then bring it down gently.

Log Hopping

When you are log hopping, the front pull and hip hop become one motion.

Perform the front pull and bring it high enough to clear the log.

Touch the front wheel on top of the log and as the front wheel starts to roll over do a hip hop.

If the log is wet avoid touching your wheels on the top of it.

Bunny Hopping

A bunny hop is similar to a log hop but with the intention of having both wheels off the ground at the same time.

Perform a front pull and whilst your front wheel is in the air use the push/pull motion to get the back wheel up.

Level your bike in the air and try to squeeze your legs together.

Land you back wheel first.

HIKING

To get the most benefit, go on long hikes and incorporate navigation training.

GENERAL HIKING TIPS

Find Your Pace

Your pace is how fast you walk. Develop a pace that you can maintain for a long time without requiring a break.

Take a series of 5 minute walks while concentrating on maintaining pace length and speed. Find a pace that slightly raises your breathing but does not make you sweat.

Walk a known distance at this pace e.g. from home to the corner store, and time how long it takes. Make the walk between 15 and 25 minutes. Repeat the same walk daily until you are covering the distance in a fairly consistent time. This is your steady pace.

Maintaining Your Pace

This is mental. Sing a song in rhythm with your steps, count your steps, breathe in time with your steps etc.

Breathing

Use slow, deliberate, deep breaths from your stomach. On flat ground use a three-to-three breathing rhythm i.e. Inhale for three steps e.g. right, left, right, then exhale for three steps.

Taking Breaks

Apart from general rest, use breaks to stretch, refuel your body, go to toilet and identify/fix any potential problems with yourself or your gear.

Unless having a meal, keep breaks short to prevent your muscles stiffening up.

Hiking with a Pack

Carry your pack with your legs. Fasten your hip belt snugly and adjust your shoulder straps so the bulk of the bag's weight rests on your hips.

Environment

Hiking is done in the elements. Watch out for dangerous plants and animals. Protect yourself from the sun. Don't freeze, overheat or dehydrate.

SPECIFIC HIKING TIPS

Uphill

Before ascending refuel your body and keep some snacks and water handy for during the climb.

Take smaller steps to maintain your pace. Avoid obstacles that require large steps.

For very steep ascents zigzagging will reduce the gradient, but adds distance.

Use a two-to-two breathing rhythm i.e. inhale for two steps and exhale for two steps.

If your pack straps are constricting you, loosen them.

Downhill

Keep your center of gravity over your legs i.e. don't lean forward or back. Stay light on your feet and keep your leg slightly bent as you plant it. Tightening your pack will improve balance.

You may be tired from the ascent, but pay attention to your foot placement.

If very steep, stand side on and lower yourself down one step at a time. Zigzagging will help to slow your pace.

Off Trail

Look for the path of least resistance. Regularly check your bearings and do not rush. If possible, do not strap things to the outside of your pack.

Crossing Water

Triple waterproof your gear. Take your hiking shoes and socks off and keep them dry.

Wider crossings usually bring shallower water, especially where ripples begin. Ripples also indicate rocks or faster flowing areas. Crossing downstream of larger rocks has less current and often an even floor.

Keep slow moving water below mid-thigh and fast moving water below the knee. Plan where you will place each step. Face slightly upstream and slide your foot forward through the water.

Use a pole on the downstream side. Place it firmly, make sure it is stable and lean on it as you step forward.

Note: Water that is deep and/or fast may pull at your poles.

If you are crossing with your pack on your back undo your hip strap and remove one shoulder. If floating your pack across, have a tether as a back-up.

If swimming across, start upstream of your exit point.

If you get swept downstream in rapids, float on your back with your feet downstream to absorb crashes. Use your hands to steer and work your way toward shore.

When in a group, put the strongest, biggest hiker on the upstream side.

Hot Weather

If possible, hike in forested land that follows a stream, or has stream crossings. Mountains are cooler than the valley.

Use electrolytes in your water, at half the strength of the recommended directions. Eat salty snacks while hiking.

Break more. Blisters will occur more readily.

Wear loose fitting clothes. Polyester is better than cotton.

Cold Weather

Use the layer system. Use thermals. Avoid cotton. Cover/uncover your head to regulate heat.

Avoid sweating. If you start warming up, slow down. When you do sweat, take off layers and replace them during breaks.

Start your hike a little cold. If after 20 minutes of hiking you are still cold, add layers.

Use sunscreen and lip balm.

Eat small amounts often and continue to rehydrate. Tubes from hydration packs can freeze.

Hiking at Altitude

High altitude hiking is trekking at an elevation that may affect your body. Some people are affected as low as 7000 feet.

Adjust your pace. Take deeper breaths and smaller steps. Perform two-to-two or one-to-one rhythmic breathing to adjust to the thinner air.

Use sunscreen and sunglasses. Weather can change quickly.

Desert Hiking

Don't count on finding water, even if marked on your map.

Watch for distant storms and beware of flash floods.

Wear light clothes that cover your whole body. Use sunscreen, sunglasses and insect repellent.

Dear Reader,

Thank you for reading **Survival Fitness.**

If you enjoyed it, please leave a review on Amazon. It helps more than most people think. You can do that here:

www.SurvivalFitnessPlan.com/Survival-Fitness-Review-Amazon

For any feedback on how to improve this or any of my books you can contact me here:

www.SurvivalFitnessPlan.com/Contact

You can claim your bonus freebies at:

www.SurvivalFitnessPlan.com/Book-Bonus-Freebies

The password is: SFPFS*%32

And you can get FREE training schedules and more by joining our newsletter:

www.SurvivalFitnessPlan.com/Free-Downloads

Thanks again for your support,

Sam Fury.

AUTHOR RECOMENDATIONS

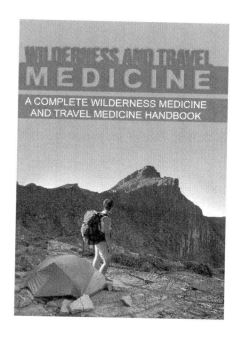

The Only Wilderness Medicine Book You Need

Discover what you need to heal yourself, because a little knowledge goes a
long way!

Get it now.

www.SurvivalFitnessPlan.com/Wilderness-Travel-Medicine

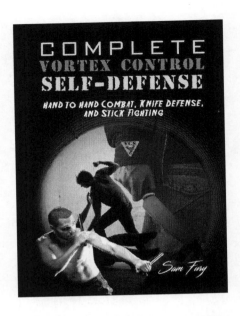

3 Self Defense Training Manuals for 1 Low Price

You'll love Vortex Control Self Defense because it is simple to learn and easy to apply.

Get it now.

www.SurvivalFitnessPlan.com/Vortex-Bundle

SURVIVAL FITNESS PLAN TRAINING MANUALS

Health and Fitness

Keep your body in optimal condition with minimal effort. The health and fitness series covers:

- **Nutrition and conditioning.** The 2 fundamentals for health and fitness.
- **Yoga.** Making Yoga a part of you daily routine will keep your mind and body healthy and in sync. Certain Yoga sequences are also a good alternative cure for many ailments.
- **Massage Therapy.** For prevention and healing of training injuries as well as general relaxation.

www.SurvivalFitnessPlan.com/Health-Fitness-Series

Survival Fitness

When in danger you have two options. Fight or Flight.

This series contains training manuals on the best methods of flight. Together with self defense, you can train in them for general health and fitness.

- **Parkour.** All the parkour skills you need to overcome obstacles in your path.
- **Climbing.** Focusing on essential bouldering techniques.
- **Riding.** Essential mountain bike riding techniques. Go as fast as possible in the safest manner.
- **Swimming.** Swimming for endurance and/or speed using the most efficient strokes.

www.SurvivalFitnessPlan.com/Survival-Fitness-Series

Self Defense

The Self Defense Series has volumes on some of the martial arts used as a base in SFP Self Defense.

It also contains the SFP Self Defense training manuals. SFP Self Defense is an efficient and effective form of minimalist self defense.

www.SurvivalFitnessPlan.com/Self-Defense-Series

Escape Evasion, and Survival

SFP escape, evasion, and survival skills (EES) focus on minimalism. It is EES using little to no special equipment.

- **Escape and Evasion.** The ability to escape capture and hide from your enemy.
- **Urban and Wilderness Survival.** Being able to live off the land in all terrains.
- **Emergency Roping.** Basic climbing skills and improvised roping techniques.
- **Water Rescue.** Life-saving water skills based on surf life-saving and military training course competencies.
- **Wilderness First Aid.** Modern medicine for use in emergency situations.

Specific subjects covered include entry and exit techniques, evasive driving, hostile negotiation tactics, lock-picking, urban survival, wilderness survival, computer hacking, and more.

www.SurvivalFitnessPlan.com/Escape-Evasion-Survival-Series

ABOUT THE AUTHOR

Sam has had an interest in self-preservation & survival for as long as he can remember. This has lead to years of training and career-related experience in related subjects.

He describes himself as a "Survivalist, Minimalist, Traveler" and spends his time exploring the world, learning new skills, and sharing his knowledge through his books.

www.SurvivalFitnessPlan.com

facebook.com/SurvivalFitnessPlan

twitter.com/Survival_Fitnes

pinterest.com/survivalfitnes

goodreads.com/SamFury

amazon.com/author/samfury

Printed in Poland
by Amazon Fulfillment
Poland Sp. z o.o., Wrocław